100 essential **embroidery** motifs

100 essential **embroidery** motifs

Susie Johns

Contents

Introduction

Welcome to this collection of designs for embroidery, where you'll find 100 different motifs, grouped into themed sections, with each one waiting for you to use your stitching skills to bring it to life.

The first chapter will introduce you to the materials and tools you'll need and how to use them, including guidance on how to prepare fabric, choose threads and use a hoop. This is followed by a chapter on stitches, which will be particularly useful for any readers that are new to embroidery.

These introductory chapters are followed by the motifs, provided in themed sections that begin with animals, which includes a menagerie of mammals and birds, plus a few insects. Next is a collection of plants, including flowers, fruit and vegetables. This is followed by a sea-themed section, then a section inspired by the home and finally a section of decorative patterns and fabulous creatures. The idea is that you will be able to find plenty to inspire you, whether you are looking for a number of related designs for a big project like a patchwork quilt or just one or two designs to use for gifts, as framed pictures or perhaps even a humble greetings card.

The motifs are provided as line drawings for you to trace straight from the page or photocopy, perhaps reducing or enlarging them as you please. There is a stitched example of each motif to inspire you and to show how various stitches can be used and combined. Each motif has been given a 'difficulty rating' of one, two or three stars; if you are new to embroidery, you can start with something straightforward with a one-star rating. Choose a simple motif such as the kangaroo, which has been outlined in easy stitches. From there you can progress to more elaborate patterns, using filling stitches and more complex colour schemes.

Bear in mind that these examples offer just one way of interpreting a motif; there are many others and you should feel free to choose your own combination of stitches, your own palette of colours and your own creative style.

Hand embroidery is a timeless craft that requires a good eye, a steady hand and just a few basic materials. It is absorbing and can be very therapeutic. You can create little gifts and treasures that people will appreciate; you can even create precious heirlooms to pass on to future generations. It all starts with a few motifs brought to life with thread. I have designed the motifs in this book inspired by the kinds of things I like to stitch and that I hope you will like as well: traditional patterns such as flowers and animals, along with some more unusual subjects to enable you to send a message or tell a story through stitching.

Tools and Materials

Embroidery requires very little in the way of materials and equipment, which means you don't have to invest much money to start this creative craft. As a basic kit, you need only a needle, some fabric, a few embroidery threads and some small, sharp scissors. In addition, an embroidery hoop will make working much easier and help to produce better results.

Fabric

It's best to use a fabric with a plain weave that is made from cotton or linen with a smooth, tightly woven texture. Both relatively inexpensive cotton and slightly more expensive linen are natural fabrics, making them a good fabric choice: a needle will glide in and out of natural fabrics more easily than it will do with synthetics. To prove this for yourself, try out some sample stitches on a piece of pure cotton or linen and then try some on a poly-cotton or other synthetic fabric.

You can, of course, buy new fabric, cut from a roll or pre-cut as fat quarters or remnants. If you choose new fabrics, it is a good idea to wash them first (see page 13). Old fabrics, sourced from charity shops, flea markets and antique fairs, donated by a friend or relative, or rescued from the linen cupboard are likely to have been washed already – probably many times – and therefore are much less likely to shrink. Of course, vintage and antique fabrics may also show signs of wear in the form of rips, stains and other flaws, so choose the cleanest examples you can find and, if necessary, position your embroidery motif carefully so it covers up any marks.

Washing new fabric

When using new natural fabrics, if they are not pre-shrunk, they should be washed and ironed before you begin stitching as they might shrink, and it is better if that happens before you embroider on them. This applies even if the finished item will be displayed as a framed picture or something similar that will not be laundered, as washing the fabric will make it softer and easier to work with, allowing the needle to glide through it more easily.

Embroidery threads

The threads are a vital component, so try to use the best threads you can afford. Cheaper versions can be rather inferior in quality: they have a tendency to break, and the dyes might run when the embroidered fabric is washed.

Six-stranded cotton embroidery thread, otherwise known as floss, has been used throughout this book and is very versatile. It is available in loosely wound skeins. You should cut a length of floss from the skein, then separate individual strands and recombine them (see also page 14). You can use any number of strands, and rarely should you be using all six. The number of strands – one, two, three, four or more – should suit the scale of the design and the weight of the fabric.

Other threads such as satin floss and perle cotton are available, but they have not been used in this book.

Choosing threads for a fabric

When working embroidery stitches on a plain weave fabric, it is important to match the weight of the thread and the thickness of the needle to the fabric. If the needle is too thick, it is likely to create holes in the fabric; if the thread is too thick, it will be difficult to pull through the fabric and the stitches will not sit neatly on the surface.

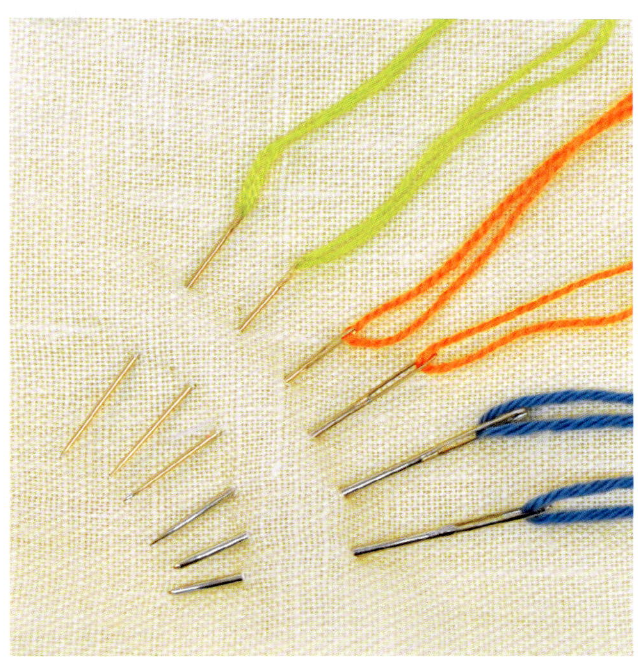

Needles

It is essential to have the right needle for embroidery. Ordinary sewing needles are not suitable, as you need a needle with a long eye to accommodate multiple strands of thread and a size that is suitable for the thickness of the fabric as well as the thread.

Crewel needles are specially designed for embroidery: these medium-length needles have a sharp point and a long eye, which makes them easier to thread. They are available in sizes 1 to 12; the smaller the number, the finer the needle. Try to use the smallest possible needle, as it will be easier to push through the fabric. Your choice will be influenced by the number of thread strands you are using. As a guideline, a size 4 or 5 will accommodate two strands of stranded cotton; for three strands you will need a size 6 or 7.

Changing needles

After a lot of use, a needle will become blunt. If you are finding it difficult to push a needle through the fabric, or if the fabric snags when you push the needle through, discard the old needle and use a new one.

Scissors

Embroidery scissors are small and have sharp, pointed blades that are essential for snipping threads and cutting away small areas of fabric. For cutting out fabric pieces, you will need a larger pair of scissors that should be reserved for cutting only fabric – never paper (which can dull the blades). Make sure you have some all-purpose scissors for cutting paper and card. Your fabric scissors should be kept sharp as blunt scissors will make cutting fabric difficult. Pinking shears have a zigzag edge that makes them useful for cutting fabrics that are liable to fray.

Pinking shears

Water Lilies (motif 26)

Embroidery hoops

A hoop consists of two wooden or plastic rings, the larger of which usually has a screw that can be tightened or loosened to accommodate fabrics of different weights or thicknesses. A hoop will hold the fabric taut, which is important when working stitches that might otherwise cause the fabric to pucker and distort.

As a general rule, stretching fabric in an embroidery hoop makes it easier to control the embroidery stitches and achieve an even tension. You can adjust each stitch as it is formed, making sure that it sits neatly on the surface of the fabric. If you work without a hoop, there can be a tendency for the thread to be pulled too tightly and the fabric to become puckered. The reason the hoop is circular is so that, while you are working stitches, you can turn the fabric in the right direction.

If the whole design does not fit completely within the hoop, it doesn't matter: the hoop can be moved around your piece of work, so there is no need to buy a hoop that is larger than your project. For the projects in this book, which are all the same scale, a 5in/12cm hoop has been used, which will accommodate the whole design in each case.

Markers

For each of the motifs in this book, you will need to mark out the design on the fabric, so you know where to place the stitches. If the stitches you are using will cover these lines completely, the lines can be drawn with some kind of permanent marker. In the examples in this book, the designs have been drawn using a ballpoint pen. These marks will remain permanent and will not bleed or fade if the fabric is washed. However, if your stitches will be more open and the design lines will show through, the lines need to be drawn with a marker that will fade or that can be removed. Some pens and pencils are suitable for making marks directly on the fabric, and some are used to transfer marks from paper to fabric using a heat source such as an iron.

An old-fashioned ballpoint (not a gel pen or rollerball) or an ordinary graphite pencil can be used to draw permanent lines. However, before using one on a project, do a test to make sure the marks are permanent. Draw some marks on a scrap of fabric using your ballpoint pen or pencil, then dampen the fabric and rub the marks with your fingertips to make sure they do not smudge or run.

Temporary markers

For making temporary marks on fabric that can later be removed, there are various pens and pencils available. The ones that fade away by themselves are the most useful for small areas of embroidery that can be finished quickly, as you don't want the marks to fade before you have had a chance to finish the stitching.

Water-erasable markers are also available. These produce marks that will last longer but can be removed with water once the embroidery is complete. For small areas, to remove the pen marks, try rubbing them with a cotton bud dampened with cold water; for larger areas, you may need to immerse the fabric in water to remove the marks. Once again, it is wise to first test them on a scrap of fabric.

Tailors' chalk pencils, some of which have a brush on the end for erasing chalk marks, are useful for marking designs on dark fabrics. Transfer pens and pencils usually leave permanent marks on fabric.

Iron

A piece of fabric that has been held in an embroidery hoop will become creased, so a steam iron is essential. Take care when pressing an embroidered piece: you should avoid squashing and flattening the stitches. Place a soft fabric such as a folded towel underneath the embroidered fabric, to provide a cushioned bed for the embroidery. Place the embroidery right side down on the soft fabric and cover it with a pressing cloth, then iron carefully. You will also need an iron if you choose to follow the heat-transfer method for transferring the motif design to fabric.

Other useful items

A tape measure is useful for measuring fabric, while a ruler is invaluable for drawing straight lines accurately. Depending on how you will be transferring the design to the fabric, you may need layout paper, a paper used by artists that is transparent but thicker than tracing paper, or you could even use bank paper, a lightweight paper used for making carbon copies.

Some embroiderers find that a thimble is a useful accessory, whereas others find it unnecessary or cumbersome. If you struggle to feed the threads through needles, you may wish to use a needle threader (see page 14).

Techniques

Once you have chosen your motif, a suitable piece of fabric and a palette of coloured threads, you are ready to start stitching. The key to a good result is to keep your stitches neat and to maintain an even tension. Here are some techniques and useful tips to help you do this, from marking out your design on the fabric to caring for your work once it's complete.

Marking designs

The easiest, quickest and most straightforward way of drawing a design onto fabric is to trace it. If you are using a lightweight fabric, when laid on top of a design it may be thin enough to see the lines through the fabric and trace them directly. With fabrics that are less translucent, you will find a light box useful for making the lines of the design visible through the fabric (see right).

As an alternative to tracing, you could make a heat transfer. For this, you will need a special transfer pen or pencil, available from embroidery material suppliers, and thin white paper such as layout paper or bank paper (but not tracing paper, which tends to cockle under the heat of the iron). Lay the paper over the design and trace it, using the transfer pen or pencil. Then lay your fabric on an ironing board, place the tracing face down on the fabric and carefully press with a hot iron. Take care that the paper's position doesn't shift as you iron or the transferred lines will be blurred. After the allotted time – check the guidelines for your particular pen or pencil – you can lift off the paper to reveal the design on the fabric.

With any direct tracing method, you will usually first need to trace or photocopy the design from the book onto plain paper. One thing you must bear in mind is that, when using the heat-transfer method, your design will be reversed. If you want it to be the right way round, you must reverse your chosen motif before tracing it.

Light boxes

By placing the motif on the light box and the fabric over it, light from the box will shine through both so you can see the lines for tracing onto the fabric. Portable LED light boxes are small, slimline and have USB connections. You can find examples that are about the size of an A4 or A3 (about 8½ x 11in/ 21.5 x 28cm or 11 x 17in/28 x 43cm) sketchbook.

If you don't have a light box, you can improvise by taping the printed design to a window on a sunny day; tape the fabric on top and you should be able to see the design and trace it onto the fabric.

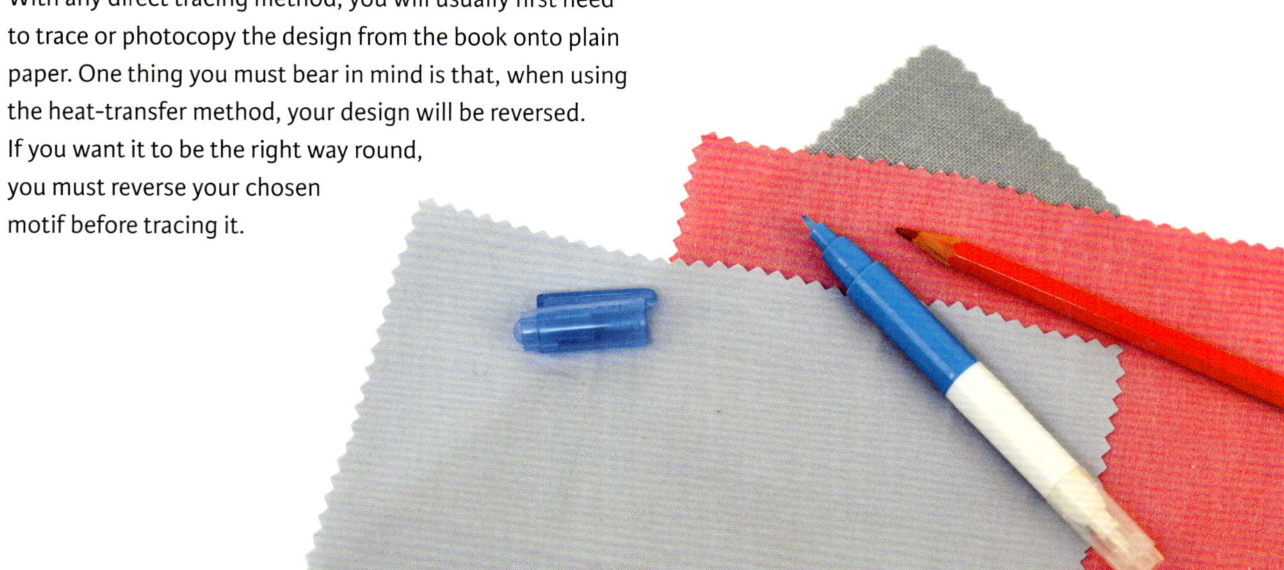

Enlarging and reducing motifs

The templates in this book are 50% scale. When they are photocopied at 200%, they will measure about 3¼–3½in (8–9cm) square – ideal for placing in the centre of a 5–6in (13–15cm) fabric square and either joined to make a decorative patchwork or framed using a square mount. Of course, there are lots of other ways to use embroidered designs: on clothing, on homeware and accessories such as curtains, tablecloths and bags, on gifts such as perfumed sachets and book covers, and on greetings cards.

To enlarge a motif

Measure the motif you wish to use, decide what size you want it to be, divide the finished size by the original size, then multiply by 100 to achieve the percentage. For example, the original motif is 2in (5cm) high and the desired size is 5in (12.5cm) high:

5 ÷ 2 = 2.5 × 100 = 250
(or 12.5 ÷ 5 = 2.5 × 100 = 250)

You will need to photocopy the motif at 250 per cent.

To reduce a motif

This is calculated in exactly the same way as enlarging; this time, the percentage you will need to photocopy at will be less than 100. For example, the original motif is 5in (12.5cm) high and the desired size is 2in (5cm) high:

2 ÷ 5 = 0.4 × 100 = 40
(or 5 ÷ 12.5 = 0.4 × 100 = 40)

You will need to photocopy the motif at 40 per cent.

Preparing the fabric

Remember that natural fabrics such as cotton or linen may shrink after washing, so you should wash it before working embroidery on it (see page 8). Regardless of whether the fabric is washed or not, it should be smooth and wrinkle-free, so press it with a hot iron before stitching to remove any creases.

Choose an embroidery hoop smaller than your piece of fabric. You will discover with practice what size of hoop feels the most comfortable and practical for you. You may wish to see the whole design within the hoop, or you may prefer to use a smaller hoop and move it to different areas of the design as you work.

So that the fabric is held firmly between the rings of the hoop, you can first bind the inner ring (see below). Place the fabric in position on the smaller innner ring, then place the other larger part of the hoop on top, pressing it down until the two parts of the ring align. You may have to loosen the screw in order for it to fit. Once in place, you will need to tighten the screw so that the fabric is held firmly in place. Tug gently on the edges of the fabric so that it is taut – but take care not to distort the fabric, as the grain should be kept straight.

The cut edges of the fabric are liable to fray, so you may wish to hem them or simply trim them with pinking shears before you start your embroidery.

Binding a hoop

Use cotton tape, bias binding or bias-cut fabric strips to wrap around the plain inner ring. Wrap one end of the fabric strip or tape around the hoop and hold it in place with a few stitches. Now wind the strip around in a diagonal fashion until you reach the starting point, then attach the end with a few more stitches.

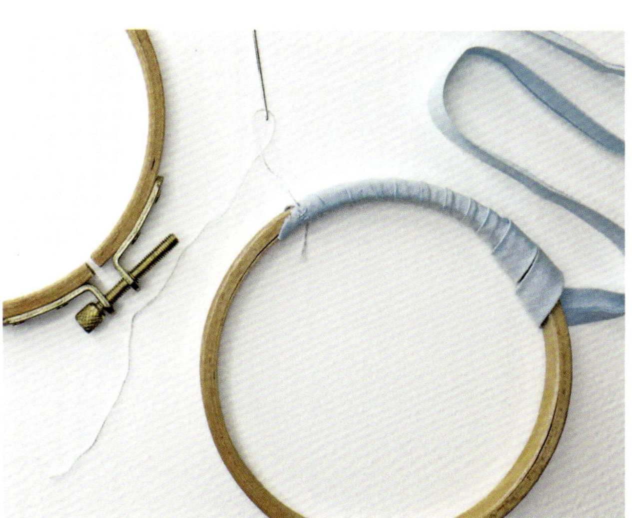

Preparing the thread

Six-stranded embroidery thread is sold in skeins, held in place with two paper bands. Do not remove these bands but hold the skein in one hand and pull on the loose end at the bottom of the skein to draw out a length of thread. Cut the length you need: an ideal length is 18–20in (45–50cm), which is more or less the length from your fingertips to your elbow. Separate this length into the number of strands you wish to use – typically, one, two or three strands, though it could be more. Separate the strands by pulling them out individually. If you try to pull out more than one at a time, they will most likely twist, then tangle and knot together.

If your skein becomes tangled, you may wish to wind the thread onto a bobbin. These are sold precisely for this purpose and are made from card or plastic. You can keep a record of the thread shade number by writing it on the bobbin, and bobbins can be stored in a box with a lid to keep them organized and dust-free. You can also make your own by punching holes along the edge of a piece of sturdy cardboard.

Six-stranded cotton embroidery thread

Threading a needle

Sometimes it can be difficult to pass the cut ends of embroidery thread through the eye of a needle, especially if you are using more than one strand. One solution is to fold the ends of the threads over the needle, pull tight, then pass the fold through the eye, instead of the cut ends themselves. Another solution is to use a needle threader

Using a needle threader

Threading a needle can sometimes be frustrating, so it is useful to keep a needle threader in your workbox. A needle threader has a wire loop that you push through the eye of the needle; you then pass the end of the thread through the loop before withdrawing the wire loop from the needle, thereby pulling the thread through the eye.

If you don't have a needle threader, you can improvise with a short length of very thin wire. Another good alternative is to use a small strip of thin paper folded in half. Cut a piece of paper about 2in (5cm) long and narrower than the eye of the needle. Fold the strip in half across its width. Place the end of the thread inside the fold and push the fold through the eye of the needle.

Using a needle threader

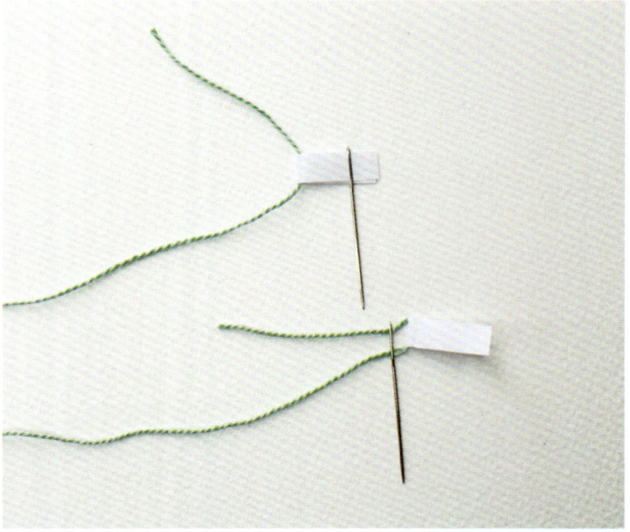

Using paper to thread a needle

Stitching techniques

There are two basic ways to insert the needle into the fabric when forming an embroidery stitch: sewing and stabbing. The method you choose is a matter of personal preference.

The sewing technique entails taking the needle in and out of the fabric in a single motion. As the needle scoops up a little of the fabric when using this method, it is usually best done without an embroidery hoop. The stabbing technique means taking the needle through the fabric from front to back, then from back to front, in two separate journeys.

When you are learning a new embroidery stitch, it is a good idea to try working it using each of the two methods to see which works best for you. The likely outcome of this type of experiment is that you will find that some stitches work better for you using the sewing technique – such as running stitch and backstitch – while others work better with the stabbing technique. You may also find that one method works best when the direction of stitching is from right to left, while the other works best going from left to right; you may even find yourself alternating the two methods while working a particular stitch.

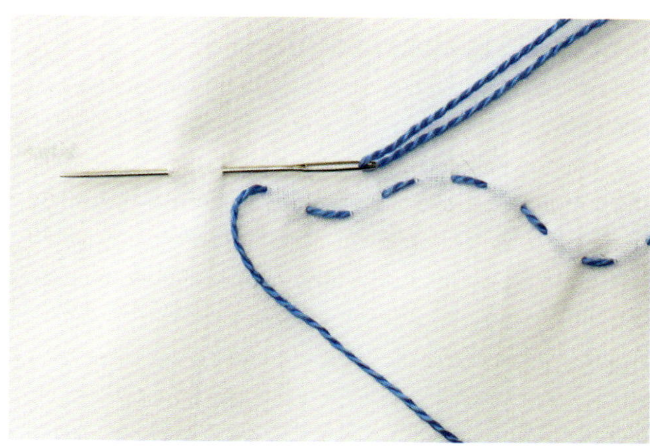

Sewing

Stabbing

Beach Huts (motif 60)

Using embroidery motifs

Each of the motifs in this book should be about 3½in (9cm) square when complete. You could place a motif in the centre of a 5in or 6in (13cm or 15cm) patchwork square and join on squares to make a patchwork project such as a cushion or quilt. You could also frame your work, using a square or rectangular mount and frame. And, of course, there are lots of other ways to use embroidered designs: on clothing, on homeware and accessories such as curtains, tablecloths and bags, on gifts such as perfumed sachets and book covers, and on greetings cards.

Fastening a thread to fabric

You can start stitching by knotting the end of the thread and inserting the needle at the first stitch, leaving the knot right next to it. However, there are several disadvantages in this method: the knot can show through on the front of the work as a little bump, it can sometimes pull through to the front of the work, and it might actually come undone, causing stitches to unravel.

There are several alternative ways to attach a new thread before starting to stitch, and one is the waste knot, which is used in this book. It entails knotting the end of the thread, then inserting the needle down through the right side of the fabric but a short distance from the design area, leaving the knot sitting on the surface of the fabric. As you start to stitch, the tail of the thread should be covered by the stitches on the wrong side, locking the thread in place. Once this thread has been secured, you can trim off the knot and any excess thread.

Of course, once you have stitched an area of the fabric, there should be no need to use the waste knot method again; new lengths of thread can be secured under the existing stitches by passing the needle back and forth under these threads two or more times.

To fasten off a length of thread when you have finished stitching, take the needle to the wrong side of the work and pass it under the back of the stitches. Make sure it is secure, with no risk of unravelling, then trim off the excess thread. To do this successfully, make sure you stop stitching before the thread becomes too short; you need to have enough thread left to enable you to take it through to the back and pass it under a sufficient number of stitches.

Aftercare

Traditionally, the advice has been to store finished embroidery pieces flat and in a dark place so that the thread colours don't fade. Where practical, you should lay your pieces unfolded in a box with layers of white acid-free tissue paper. Larger pieces can be rolled around a cardboard tube covered with tissue, right side out, then over-wrapped with more tissue.

Of course, not all embroidery projects should be stored away. Hopefully, you will want to frame your finished work or perhaps to make it into a cushion or other item that will be on show. The fabric and threads may fade over time, but in the meantime you will have the opportunity to enjoy looking at your handiwork and allowing others to do so too.

Waste knot

Fastening off

Choosing Colours

Embroidery thread is available in a dazzling selection of colours. For the examples in this book, a palette of fifty DMC colours, plus black and white, was used, but you can substitute your own favourite brand. The colours listed in the patterns are just suggestions – the motifs will look stunning whatever colour you choose.

	666	red
	347	russet
	891	watermelon
	608	flame
	740	orange
	741	tangerine
	742	apricot
	444	yellow
	307	buttermilk
	907	lime
	703	shamrock
	701	emerald
	943	pine green
	991	jade
	995	turquoise
	3846	aqua
	799	cornflower
	322	French blue
	798	royal blue
	340	lavender
	208	violet
	553	grape
	3607	red-violet
	3806	fuchsia
	335	pomegranate

	894	candy pink
	760	salmon
	353	blush
	3341	peach
	783	mustard
	869	cocoa
	918	chestnut
	746	ivory
	3046	beige
	16	celery
	988	sage
	702	fern
	563	pistachio
	927	grey
	3810	sea green
	800	sky blue
	436	cappuccino
	645	dark grey
	840	sepia
	642	stone
	3042	heather
	210	lilac
	3609	heliotrope
	956	rose pink
	605	shell pink

Stitch Guide

There are many different embroidery stitches but here are just a handful – the ones used to stitch the examples throughout the book – to keep things simple. Some stitches – mostly those that form narrow lines – are used for outlining, while others are used for filling. It's a bit like painting with thread.

Whatever motif you decide to embroider, you will need to choose suitable stitches. These motifs are designed to be worked on plain-weave fabric, using a type of embroidery known as surface embroidery, or freestyle. Most of the stitches are worked without much regard to the weave of the fabric and, unlike other embroidery techniques such as canvaswork, blackwork, hardanger and counted cross stitch, the stitches you make for these motifs can be large or small, and you can make them in any direction.

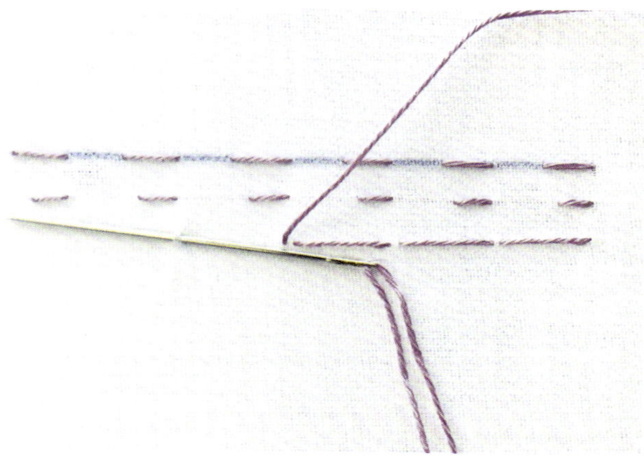

Running stitch

The most basic embroidery stitch is also one of the most versatile and popular. It really is the easiest stitch of all to work. If you are working this stitch in a hoop, use a stabbing motion (see page 15), take the needle up through the fabric and pull the thread taut before you push it back down through the fabric, completing one stitch at a time. If you are working without a hoop, you can work several stitches at a time, using a rocking motion to take the needle in and out of the fabric at a shallow angle.

Running stitch can be used to outline shapes. Working from right to left, bring the needle up to the surface, then back down into the fabric a little way along the stitch line and up again about the same distance along; repeat this action all along the line. It can also be used as padding under satin stitch, especially where a dark thread is used on a light-coloured fabric.

Straight stitch

This simply describes a single stitch, worked in isolation – for example, to suggest a flower stamen or blade of grass. It's so simple, it hardly merits a separate entry, but this stitch should not be underestimated as it forms the foundation of other stitches, such as running stitch. It is sometimes called single satin stitch.

Bring the needle up through the fabric and back down a stitch length away. Pull the thread through to create a single straight stitch.

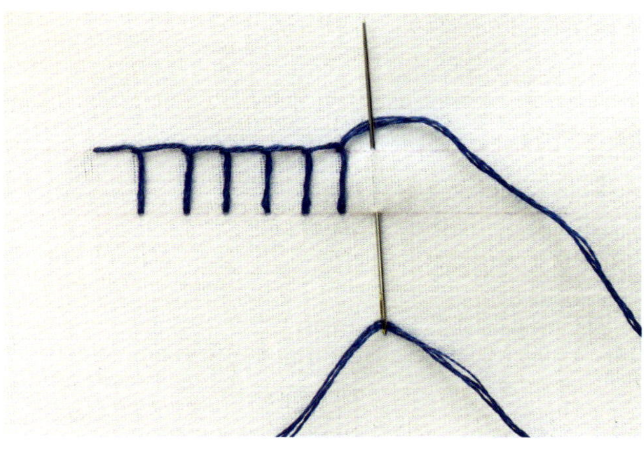

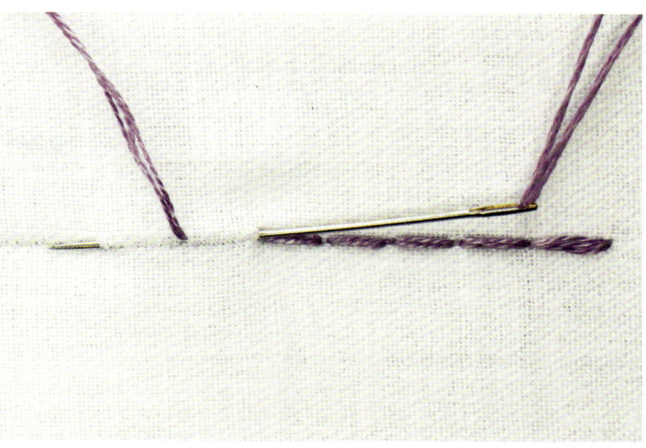

Blanket stitch

This is used as a decorative stitch in motifs, but it can also be used to strengthen the edges of thick fabrics such as blankets – hence the name.

Bring the needle up through the fabric on the line. Insert it a little way to the right and below the line, then back up through the upper line immediately above, making sure that the loop of thread is behind the needle; pull it through to make the first stitch, then, working from left to right, repeat the process, taking the needle down through the fabric below the line and up on the line, creating a small loop each time and spacing the stitches evenly.

Buttonhole stitch

This is executed in exactly the same way as blanket stitch but with stitches worked closely together.

Backstitch

You can use backstitch to describe straight lines, wavy lines and curves. It is useful for outlining around the edge of a shape and looks good in combination with most other embroidery stitches. Backstitch is useful for outlining light-coloured areas that might not otherwise show up against the background fabric. As its name implies, each stitch involves bring the thread back a little from the original entry point before finishing the stitch further in front of it.

Working from right to left, bring the needle up through the fabric a little to the left of the beginning of the line to be worked. Now insert the needle back down through the fabric at the beginning of the line (to the right of the first point) and up again a stitch length in front of the place the needle first emerged. Repeat the process, going back in again at the starting point of the previous stitch, then forward, a stitch length in front.

Split stitch

As well as being a useful outlining stitch, rows of split stitch can be worked close together as a filling stitch (see page 23).

Working from left to right, bring the needle up at the beginning of the line to be worked, then down a stitch length to the right. Pull the thread through to form the first stitch, then bring the needle up through the centre of the stitch. Repeat along the length of the line.

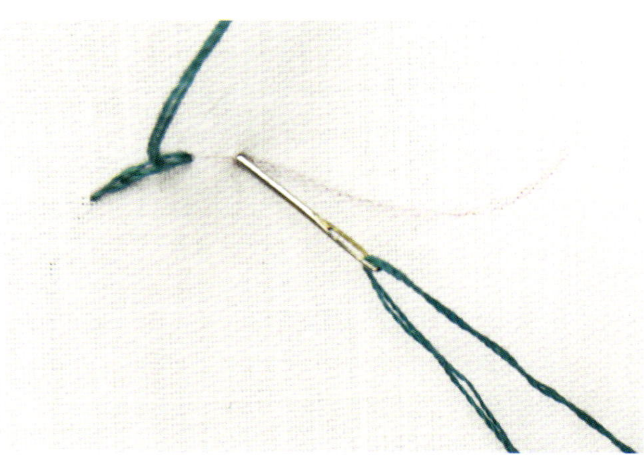

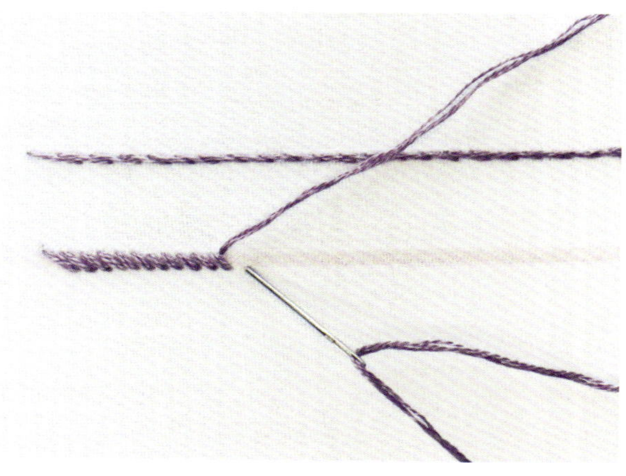

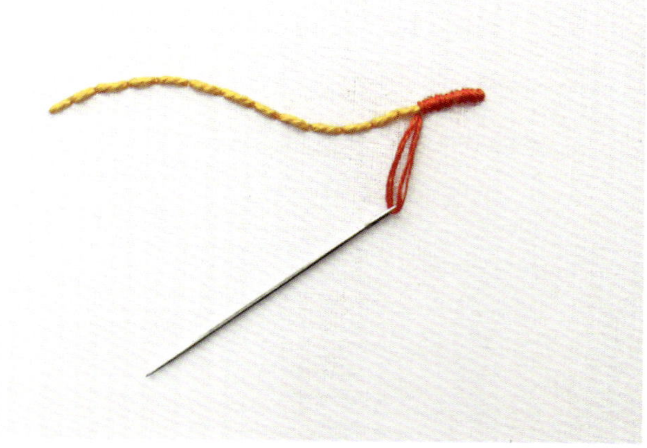

Stem stitch and raised stem stitch

As the name implies, this stitch is useful for embroidering stems. It also makes a good, solid outline. You can vary the width of the line and you can work stem stitch over a line of backstitch to raise it slightly.

Working from left to right, bring the needle up at the beginning of the line to be worked, then down a stitch length to the right. Pull the thread through to form the first slanted stitch. Bring the needle up just above the centre of the first stitch and along the line, to the right, another stitch length. Repeat the process along the length of the line. You can vary the length of the stitches and the slant to make a thinner or thicker line. The thread has a tendency to twist as you create stem stitches, so dangle the needle from time to time to allow the thread to untwist.

For raised stem stitch, work a line of backstitch, then start again at the beginning and work stem stitch over the top.

Overcast stitch

This creates a smooth raised line, like a very fine cord, when worked over a line of backstitch (or sometimes close running stitch or split stitch). It is useful for creating stems and bold outlines.

Start by working backstitch along the lines. Now bring the needle up close to the foundation backstitches, at any point on the outline, just inside the line. Take the needle back down through the fabric on the opposite side of the outline, and back up on the inside of the line, close to the previous stitch. Continue like this, working over the foundation line, to create a neat, cord-like stitch. Make sure the stitches are worked close together and that the foundation stitches are completely covered.

Long-and-short stitch

This variation of satin stitch can be used to cover larger shapes. It can also be worked in several colours or different shades of the same colour. Take the needle in and out of the fabric just outside the outline of the shape to be filled, so that lines are covered by the stitches.

Work the first row in alternating long and short stitches. Work the second and subsequent rows in stitches that are all the same length as each other, taking the needle into the end of the stitch above, so that alternate stitches will be offset, or 'stepped'.

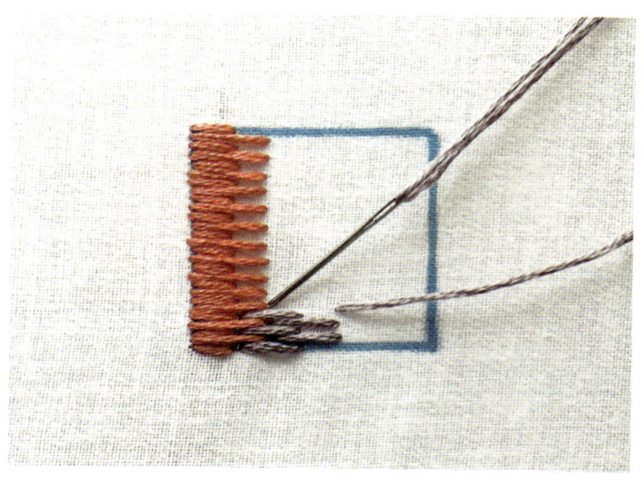

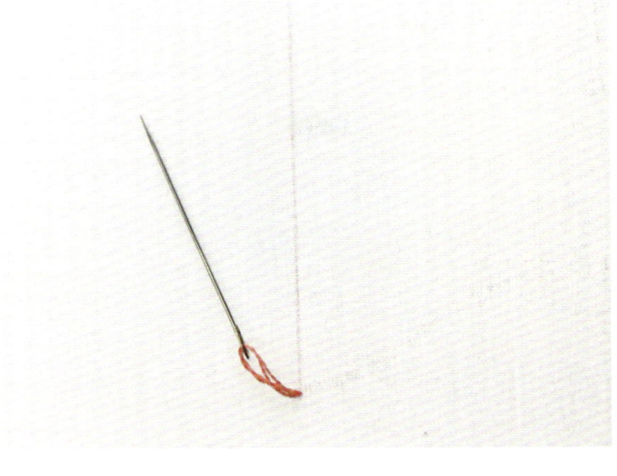

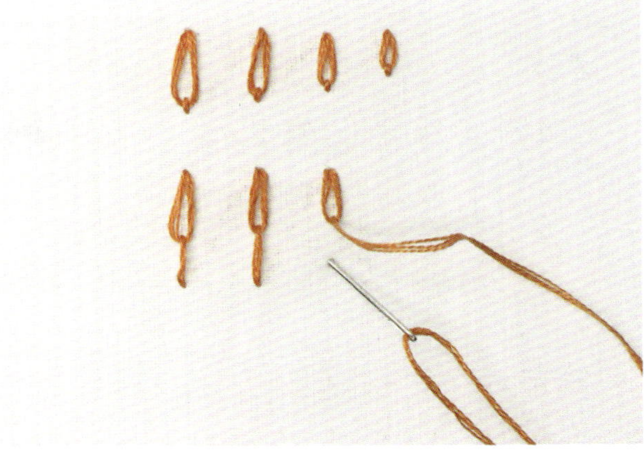

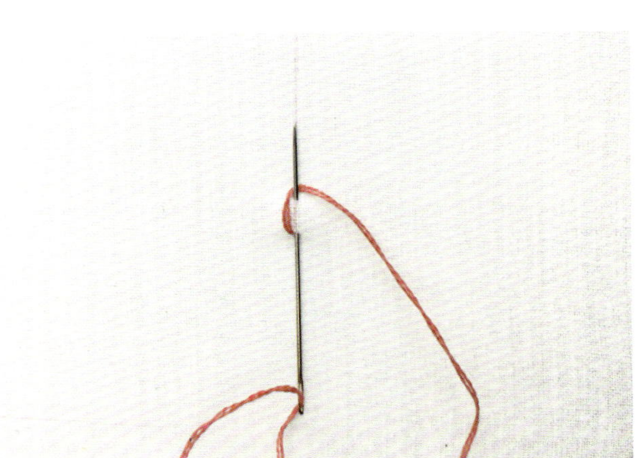

Detached chain stitch

This stitch is traditionally used to form single petals that can be arranged to form a simple daisy motif – hence its nickname of 'lazy daisy' stitch.

Bring the needle up through the fabric and insert it again into the same place. Pull it through, creating a small loop of thread. Bring the tip of the needle up through the loop and pull through, then re-insert it down through the fabric, trapping the loop with a small straight stitch.

Chain stitch

These cleverly linked stitches create a line that resembles a chain. This is a versatile stitch that can used to describe straight or curved lines. Rows of chain stitch can also be worked close together as a filling (this is chain stitch filling).

Working from top to bottom, bottom to top, or right to left, whichever is most comfortable, bring the needle up at the beginning of the line to be worked, then back down at the same point and out again a stitch length along the line, with the tip of the needle under the loop of thread. Pull the thread through to form the first stitch, then take the needle back down through the loop of the first stitch and out again a stitch length along the line, with the tip of the needle under the loop of thread once again. Repeat along the length of the line to create a chain of linked loops. To finish off the line, secure the last loop of the chain with a short stitch, taking the needle to the back of the work; fasten off.

Figs (motif 36)

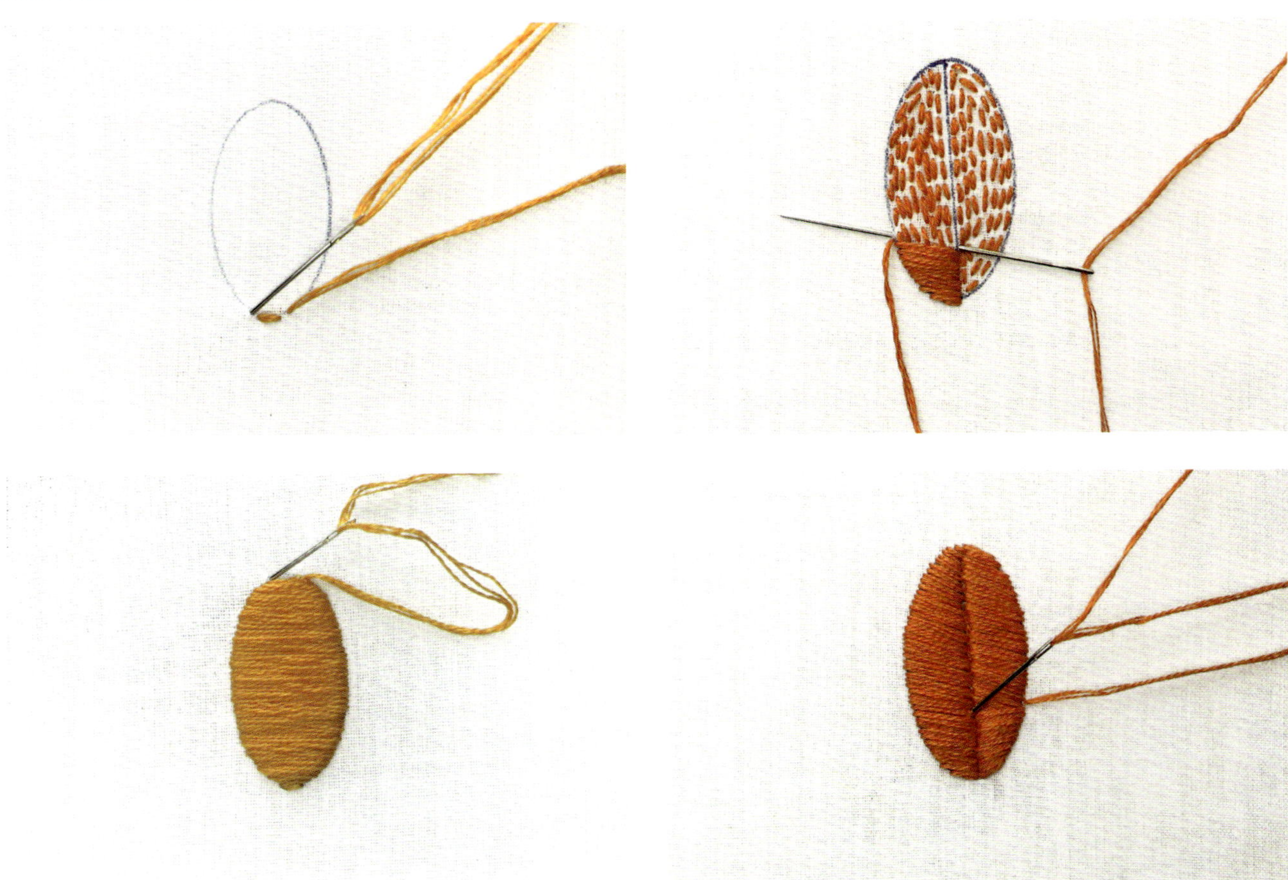

Satin stitch and padded satin stitch

Satin stitch is used to fill areas so that the fabric beneath does not show through. Stitches are usually parallel, with no gaps between them, creating a solid area of colour. For curved shapes, you may wish to fan out the stitches instead of working them parallel. In all cases, stitches should be kept quite short so they do not snag or pull, so make sure that shapes to be filled are quite small. (For larger shapes, use long-and-short stitch instead; see page 20.)

Take the needle in and out of the fabric just outside the outline of the shape to be filled, so that all the design lines are covered by the stitches. Working from right to left, or from bottom to top if you find it easier, bring the needle up through the fabric on the right side of the shape, just outside the drawn line, then down into the fabric on the left. Pull the thread through, then bring the needle back out on the right-hand side of the shape, right next to the first stitch. Repeat this process, keeping the stitches close together and covering the drawn outline.

Where you are working with a dark-coloured thread on a light-coloured fabric or a light thread on dark fabric, you may wish to fill the inside of the shape first with rows of running stitch in the same coloured thread, which will help to create a more solid colour. You can also fill the shape more thickly with thread before working over it with satin stitch, to create a slightly padded effect.

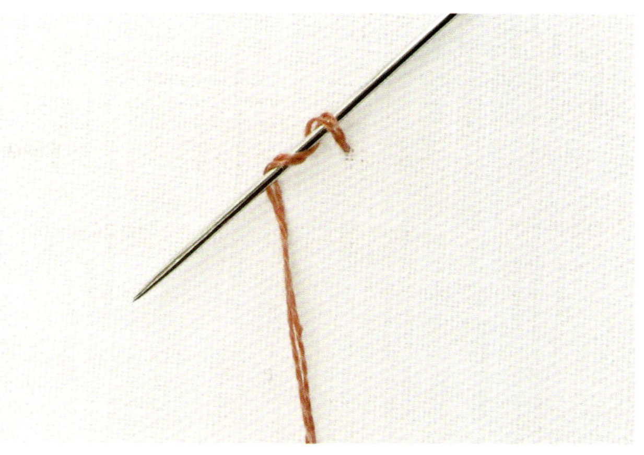

Split stitch filling and split stitch shading

Split stitch proves its versatility when used as a filling stitch. You can alter the stitch length, change colours and work the rows of stitches to follow quite intricate shapes and contours. When a single colour is used to fill a shape, it's usually referred to as split stitch filling, and when colours are changed within a shape to form a blended transition from one to another, it's split stitch shading.

Working from left to right, bring the needle up onto the outline of the shape to be filled, then down a stitch length to the right. Pull the thread through to form the first stitch, then bring the needle back to the left and up through the centre of the stitch. Repeat this along the length of the line. Now work from right to left – or turn the work to allow you to work from left to right – and make another line of split stitch close to the first. Offset the stitches so that the centres and ends do not line up. For a shaded effect, change colours where appropriate to form subtle gradations of colour.

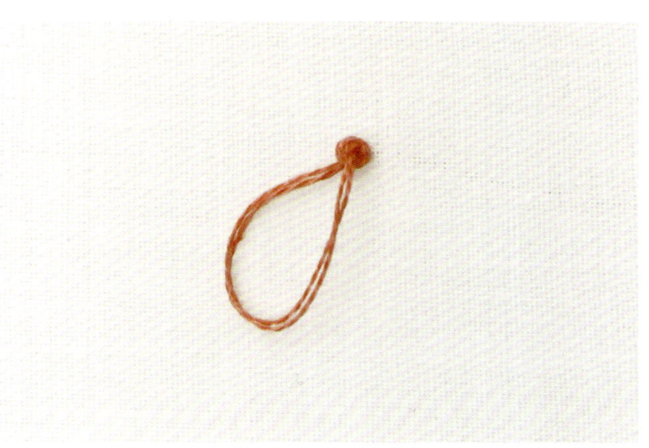

French knot

This forms a neat knot on the surface of the fabric, like a small seed, perfect for flower centres and pupils in eyes.

Bring the needle up through the fabric at the point you wish to place the knot and twist the tip of the needle one, two or three times around the thread where it emerges from the fabric. With the twists held tightly, insert the tip of the needle close to where it first emerged and pull through, holding the twists and allowing a small knot to form on the surface of the fabric. The number of twists will determine the size of the knot: for a larger knot, do not add more twists but use a thicker thread.

Motif 1: Butterflies

With lots of potential for using colour creatively, here's one large and one small butterfly. Use one or both, and repeat them to your heart's desire.

Thread colours

- 645 dark grey
- 642 stone
- 891 watermelon
- 927 grey
- 995 turquoise
- B5200 white
- 3846 aqua
- 907 lime
- 608 flame
- 741 tangerine
- 444 yellow

Use two strands of thread throughout, unless otherwise stated.

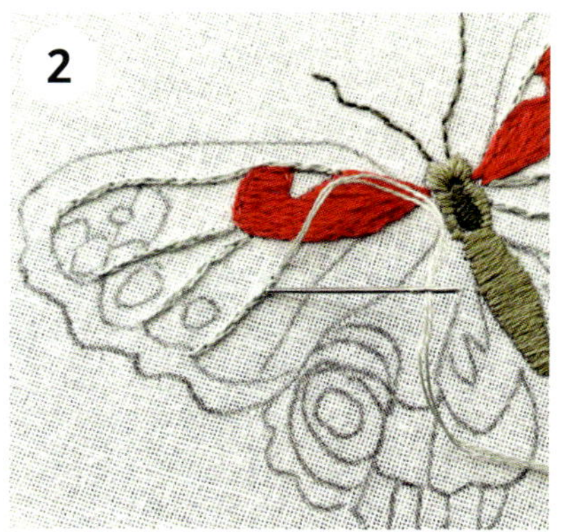

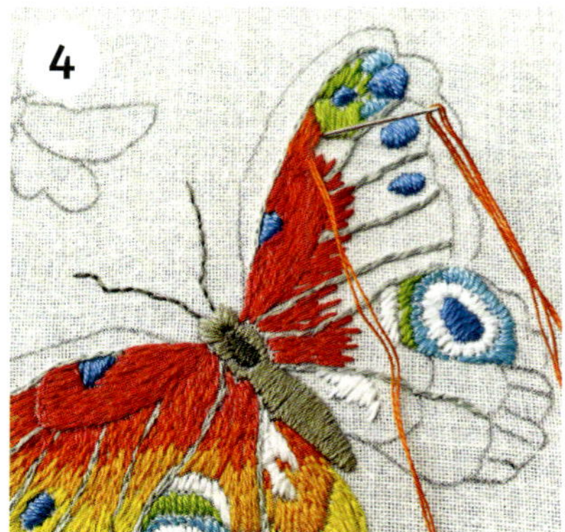

1. Fill in the spot on the body of the larger butterfly in satin stitch, using 645, then define the antennae using a single strand in backstitch. Fill in the rest of the body in 642.
2. Fill in the two petal shapes on the upper wings in 891 and split stitch filling. Define the lines across the wings using split stitch and 927.
3. Fill in the spots on the wings with satin stitch and 995, B5200, 3846 and 907.
4. Now fill in the surrounding areas using split stitch shading, with 608 blending into 741, then blending into 444.
5. Complete the outer borders of the wings in satin stitch, using 907 for the upper wings and 3846 for the lower ones.
6. For the smaller butterfly, fill in the body using satin stitch and 927 then thread the needle with one strand of 927 and one strand of 3846, then fill in the wings with split stitch filling.

Notes on technique

Split stitch filling is a good technique for creating blends or graduations of different colours, sometimes called ombré.

Motif 2:
Frog

For a pop of colour, you can choose a bright contrasting shade for the frog's feet. Or you could go for a more subtle camouflage colour scheme, if you prefer.

Thread colours

- 702 fern
- 907 lime
- 891 watermelon
- B5200 white
- 310 black

Use two strands of thread throughout, unless otherwise stated.

1. Using 702, fill in the eyelids with satin stitch, then follow the forked line down the centre of the frog with chain stitch.
2. Fill in the body and head with 907, using split stitch filling. Still using split stitch filling, fill in the legs: use 907 for the top third of each leg, one strand each of 907 and 702 for the centre section, and 702 for the rest.
3. Use 891 and satin stitch for the feet, and for the eyes use B5200 and 310.

Notes on technique

Though just two shades of green have been used to fill in this frog's body, head and legs, by cleverly combining two colours in the needle at the same time in places, you can create subtle blended effects, which is sometimes referred to as a melange.

Motif 3:
Dragonfly

With long bodies and two pairs of intricately veined wings, these dainty creatures are colourful, offering plenty of scope for creativity. Common names for the dragonfly include devil's arrow and devil's darning needle.

Thread colours

- 995 turquoise
- 310 black
- 907 lime
- 307 buttermilk
- 3609 heliotrope
- 3846 aqua
- 894 candy pink
- 210 lilac

Use two strands of thread throughout, unless otherwise stated.

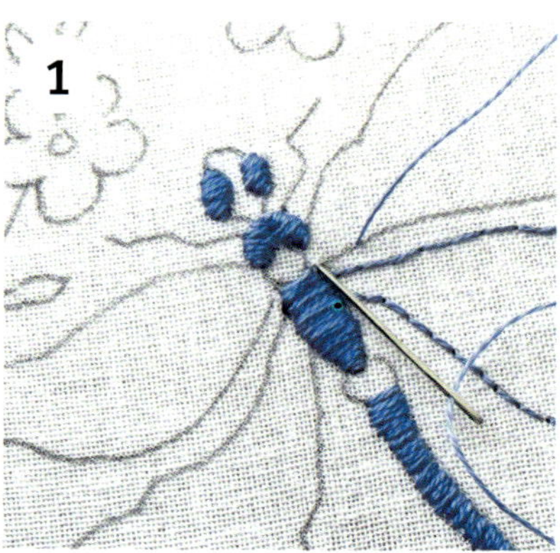

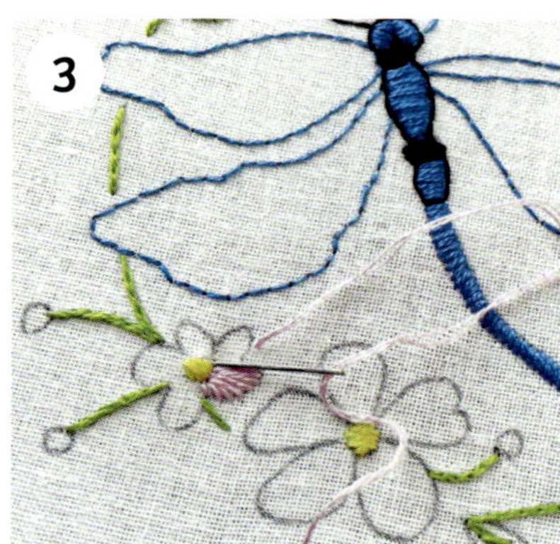

1. Using two strands of 995, fill in the dragonfly's tail and alternate sections of the body in satin stitch, as well as the eyes. Now use a single strand of the same colour to outline the wings in backstitch.
2. With two strands of 310, fill in the rest of the body with satin stitch, then outline the body and the legs with a single strand, using backstitch.
3. For the floral border, use two strands of thread throughout. Use 907 and split stitch for the stems; satin stitch for the leaves. Use satin stitch for the flowers: 307 for the flower centres and 3609 for the petals and buds.
4. For the vein pattern on the wings, use a single strand and three colours: 3846, 894 and 210. Fill in the whole area of each wing with rows of open chain stitches to create a honeycomb effect.

Notes on technique

Clever use of chain stitch creates a veined pattern on the dragonfly's wings. This, combined with colour changes, adds a delicacy appropriate to the subject.

Motif 4:
Spider

This motif features the spider's web rather than the spider itself – though you will find it lying in wait within the web. Completed in backstitch, with a satin stitch spider, this is the easiest motif in the book, making it ideal for embroidery beginners.

Thread colours

- 800 sky blue
- 642 stone
- 310 black

Use two strands of thread throughout.

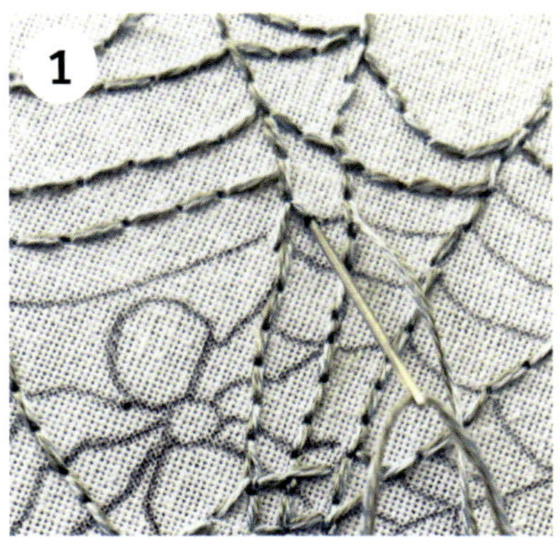

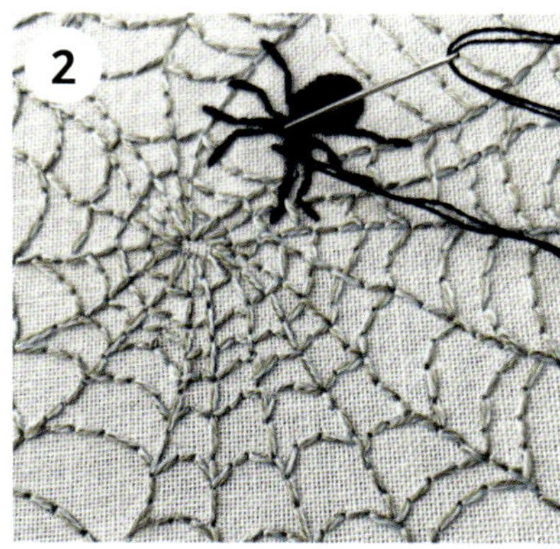

1. Thread your needle with one strand of 800 and one strand of 642 and follow the lines of the web using backstitch.
2. With two strands of 310, fill in the spider's body using satin stitch. Now add legs using backstitch.

Notes on technique

If you wish to make the strands of the spiderweb thicker, embroider them in split stitch instead of backstitch. For a finer web, use a single strand of embroidery thread.

Motif 5:
Owl

For many people, an owl represents wisdom. Some people also consider them to be a sign of good luck.

Thread colours

- 310 black
- 444 yellow
- 436 cappuccino
- 642 stone
- 3046 beige
- 746 ivory
- 840 sepia
- 783 mustard
- 645 dark grey
- 703 shamrock

Use two strands of thread throughout.

1. Using satin stitch, fill in the eye centres in 310 and the rings around the centres in 444. Outline these rings with 310 and backstitch, then fill the outer ring with 436.
2. Still using satin stitch, fill in the beak with 642 and the rest of the face with 3046.
3. Next, thread the needle with one strand of 840 and one strand of 436, and embroider the 'eyebrows' using satin stitch. Fill in the section above with 3046 and the top of the head with 840.
4. For the chest feathers, thread the needle with one strand of 3046 and one strand of 746. Starting on the top row, fill individual feathers with satin stitch, working the stitches horizontally, then outline the underside of the feathers with two rows of split stitch in 783. Repeat this filling and outlining process, row by row, working down the whole chest.
5. For the wings, use a combination of 840 and 436 to fill the shapes using satin stitch, and 645 for outlining in split stitch and for the feet using satin stitch.
6. Fill in the branch with satin stitch using 436. Finally, fill the leaves using 703 and satin stitch.

Motif 6:
Penguins

Standing in an icy landscape, here is a cute pair of penguins: one is viewed from behind, while the other faces front.

Thread colours

- B5200 white
- 307 buttermilk
- 444 yellow
- 741 tangerine
- 310 black
- 740 orange
- 800 sky blue

Use two strands of thread throughout.

1. Starting with the right-hand penguin, fill in the lower section of the body with close rows of chain stitch, using B5200.
2. Now, in the chest area and using long-and-short stitch, fill it with 307 for the lower row, 444 for the middle row and 741 for the upper row.
3. Fill in the eye using B5200 and add a pupil in 310 by making a small French knot. Fill in the beak with 740 and the stripe on the head with 741, using satin stitch for both, then switch to 310 and fill in the rest of the head, body and wings, continuing to use satin stitch.
4. For the other penguin, fill in the body and neck with long-and-short stitch, using 310, then complete the head, beak, wings and feet to match the first penguin.
5. Finally, for the icy landscape, use 800 and blanket stitch, with the top of the stitch following the lines.

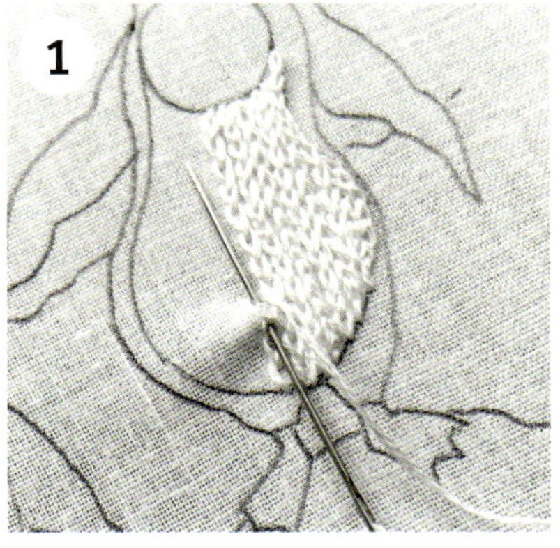

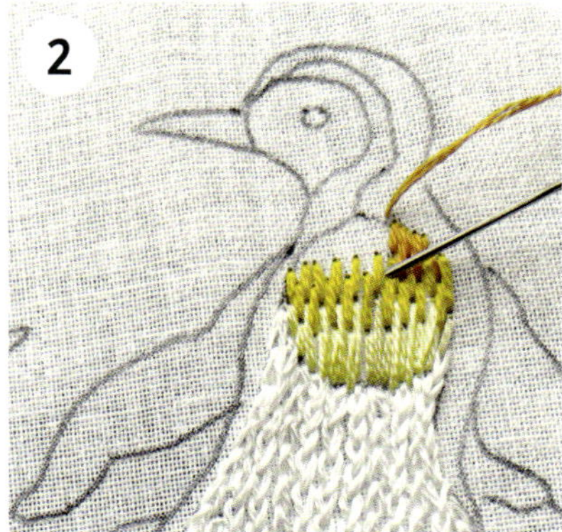

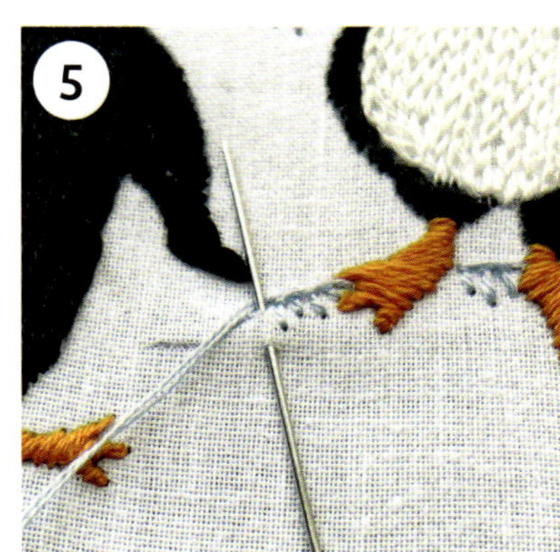

Motif 7:
Flamingo

With their characteristic pink colour and their ability to stand on one leg, these wading birds represent beauty, balance and grace. A group of flamingoes is called a flamboyance.

Thread colours

- B5200 white
- 760 salmon
- 310 black
- 3806 fuchsia
- 894 candy pink
- 605 shell pink
- 3042 heather
- 3846 aqua
- 943 sea green

Use two strands of thread throughout.

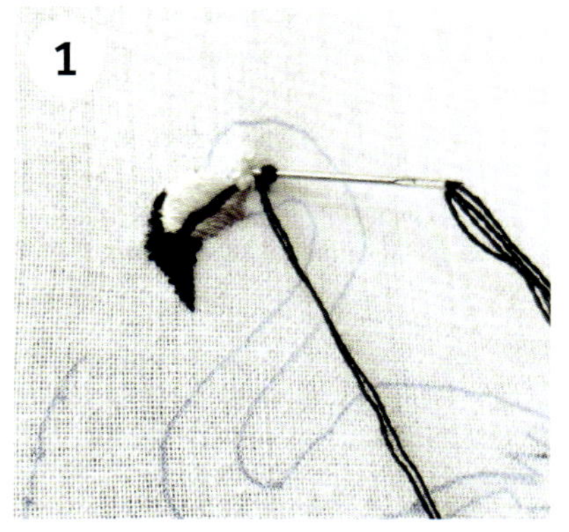

1. Fill in the top of the beak and the eye in satin stitch and B5200, then fill in the lower section of the beak with 760 and the front with 310. Still using 310, add a French knot in the centre of the eye.
2. Use 3806 and split stitch filling for the head, following the contours of the shape and transitioning into satin stitch as you move down the neck.
3. Thread the needle with one strand each of 3806 and 894 and start filling in the top of the body with split stitch filling, then change to two strands of 894 to complete it.
4. For the lower section, continue with satin stitches, using one strand of 605 and one of 760; then use two strands of 3806 for the centre segment and 605 for the tail feathers.
5. Embroider the legs using 3042; first make a foundation of backstitch and then cover it with overcast stitch.
6. For the water, use split stitch and 3846. For the plants, use 943, with split stitch for the stems and detached chain stitches for the leaves.

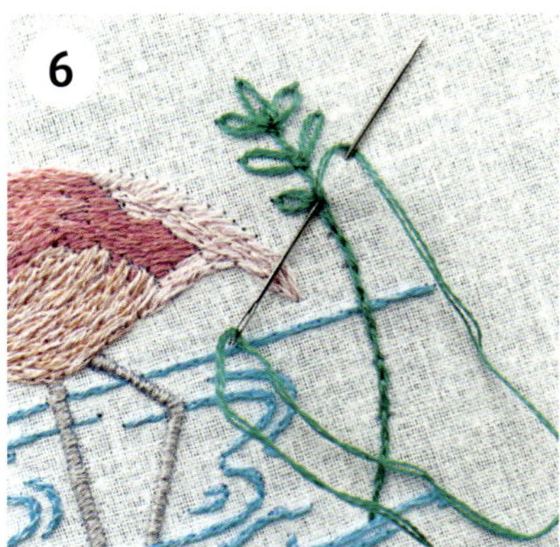

Notes on technique

When tracing the motif onto fabric, just draw the stems and not the whole leaves, with small marks at regular intervals to indicate the position of each leaf.

Motif 8: Chickens

Here you have the perfect companions for the Cockerel on page 34, with plenty of scope for choosing your own colour palette for the pretty feathers.

Thread colours

- 444 yellow
- 891 watermelon
- 645 dark grey
- 918 chestnut
- 347 russet
- 3046 beige
- 436 cappuccino
- 783 mustard
- 840 sepia
- 642 stone
- 307 buttermilk
- 703 shamrock

Use two strands of thread throughout, unless otherwise stated.

1. Using 444, fill in the beak and eye using satin stitch. Using 891, fill in the comb and wattle, also in satin stitch.
2. Fill in the area from the top of the head to just below the eye with split stitch filling and 645. Now change to a combination of one strand of 918 and one strand of 347 and make close rows of chain stitch to fill in the rest of the head.
3. Use 3046 to fill the area above the wing with split stitch filling and then 436 to fill in the areas on the breast and thighs.
4. For the top of the wing, use one strand of 918 and one strand of 347 and chain stitch once again, then fill in the wing feathers with 783 and satin stitch, working each feather separately with the stitches laid across the width.
5. For the base of the tail, use 840 and split stitch filling and for the tail feathers use the 918 and 347 combination and chain stitch. Finish the hen by using 642 and overcast stitch for the chicken's legs.
6. For the chicks, fill in the wings and beaks using satin stitch and 444, and the bodies and heads using split stitch filling and 307. Use a single strand of 645 to outline the beaks with split stitch and add a French knot to the centre of the eyes.
7. Finally, embroider the grass in split stitch with two strands of 703.

Notes on technique

By combining two colours in the needle, you can create interesting shaded effects, and using a combination of different stitches and changing the direction of the stitches will create interesting textures.

Motif 9: Cockerel

A cockerel is a young male chicken; an adult male is a cock or a rooster. You can decide which of these is depicted here. They have longer tail feathers than chickens and often display very colourful plumage.

Thread colours

- 310 black
- 608 flame
- 666 red
- 741 tangerine
- 991 jade
- 918 chestnut
- 347 russet
- 322 French blue
- 3810 sea green
- 335 pomegranate
- 702 fern
- 444 yellow

Use two strands of thread throughout, unless otherwise stated.

1. Using satin stitch, fill in the centre of the eye with 310, the eye surround with 608, and the comb and wattle with 666.
2. Using split stitch filling, fill in the head shape with 741, the front of the breast and the tops of the legs with 991, and the top of the wing using a combination of one strand of 918 and one strand of 347.
3. Fill in the wing feathers with 741 and satin stitch. Next, fill in the rest of the body with split stitch filling using one strand of 322 and one strand of 3810 combined.
4. Complete the tail with satin stitch, using the 918 and 347 combination for the first layer of feathers and 991 for the long feathers.
5. Embroider the feet with 335, also in satin stitch. Finally, use split stitch and 702 for the flower stems, and 444 and 608 for the flowers, using satin stitch.

Creative ideas

Pair the cockerel with the chickens from page 33 to decorate a tea cosy, or repeat them along the hem of a kitchen curtain.

Motif 10:
Parrot

Parrots are to be found in trees in dense forests. This one is perching on a leafy branch, just waiting to be captured in colourful threads.

Thread colours

- 746 ivory
- 741 tangerine
- B5200 white
- 310 black
- 666 red
- 608 flame
- 444 yellow
- 995 turquoise
- 645 dark grey
- 436 cappuccino
- 702 fern

Use two strands of thread throughout, unless otherwise stated.

1. Using satin stitch, fill in the areas of the central part of the head: the cheek with 746 and 741, then the eye with B5200, the upper beak with 746 and the lower beak with 310. Use 310 to outline the eye in backstitch and use a tiny straight stitch for the pupil; use satin stitch to define the upper beak. Now use a single strand of 666 to add broken stripes in running stitch across the face.
2. Complete the head using 666 and satin stitch, changing the direction of the stitches as you follow the contours of the head. Fill in the rows of feathers on the breast and abdomen with satin stitch using 608 and 666 alternately.
3. Still using satin stitch, fill in the tops of the wings with 666, the middle part with 444 and the lower feathers with 995. For the claws, use 645.
4. Still using satin stitch, fill in the branch using 436, then complete the tail feathers using 995. For the smaller twigs, use stem stitch, then fill in the leaves in 702 and satin stitch.

Creative ideas

You don't have to use the colours shown here – this is just one illustration of how you could fill in the motif. You could also break up the head into different sections according to the type of parrot you wish to depict.

Motif 11:
Budgerigar

Budgies are popular pets. The natural colour of this small Australian parakeet is green, but it has been bred in a variety of hues, including blue, white, yellow and grey.

Thread colours

- B5200 white
- 3846 aqua
- 310 black
- 307 buttermilk
- 760 salmon
- 645 dark grey
- 436 cappuccino
- 563 pistachio

Use two strands of thread throughout, unless otherwise stated.

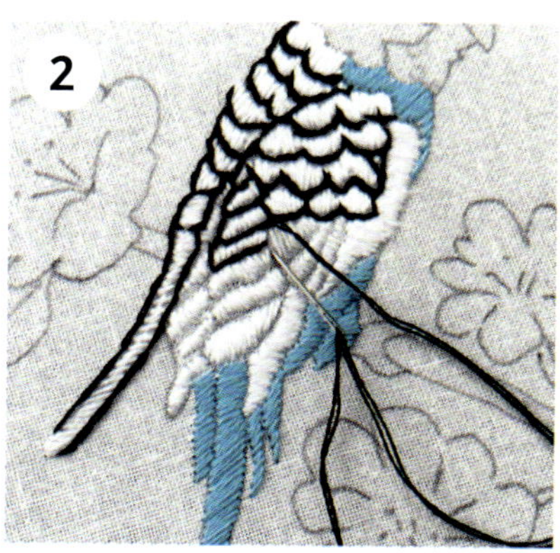

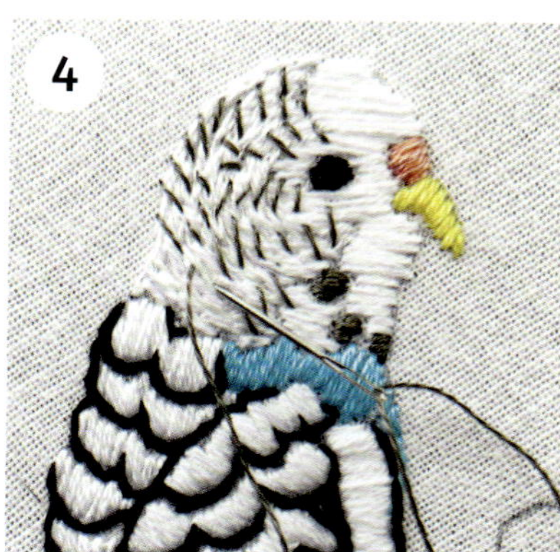

1. Using B5200 and starting at the top of the wing, fill in the scalloped shapes with satin stitch, taking the needle through the fabric just inside the lines, so that they remain visible. Still using satin stitch, fill in the breast and the tail feathers in 3846.
2. With split stitch and 310, outline the wing feathers. Make some of the outlines heavier in places by working extra stitches.
3. Fill in the eye in 310 and satin stitch, then complete the head in B5200 using satin stitch for the front part and split stitch filling for the back, working the lines of stitches to follow the round contours of the head shape.
4. Fill in the beak in satin stitch, using 307. Using the same stitch and 760, now fill in the little ridge above the beak – the cere – and the foot. With a single strand of 645, add lines of running stitch on top and for filling in the throat spots.
5. Fill in the branch in satin stitch, using 436, then outline the flowers in split stitch, using 760, and make the flower centres in split stitch and French knots, using 307. Fill in the leaves with satin stitch in 563.

Motif 12: Peacock

A peacock, with his resplendent tail, is the male of the species. This one has his tail down, as he fits the format better that way.

Thread colours

- 3846 aqua
- 995 turquoise
- 783 mustard
- 991 jade
- 927 grey
- 943 pine green
- 798 royal blue
- 310 black

Use two strands of thread throughout.

1. Using 3846, stitch a detached chain stitch over each dot on the tail feathers. Now, with 995, fill the centre of each chain with a single small straight stitch.
2. Use satin stitch and 783 to fill in the ovular shape surrounding each chain stitch and stitch along the quills with stem stitch. Complete the feathers with 991 and satin stitch, making a few longer stitches around the ends to create a more feathery effect.
3. Using satin stitch and 927, fill in the wings, beak and eye.
4. Starting at the base of the tail, fill in the body above the wing using 943 and satin stitch and continue across the neck, where you should change to long-and-short stitch. Change to 798 for the front of the bird and continue halfway down.
5. With 927, embroider the legs and crest using split stitch. Finally, add French knots to the top of the crest using 995 and a French knot in 310 for the eye.

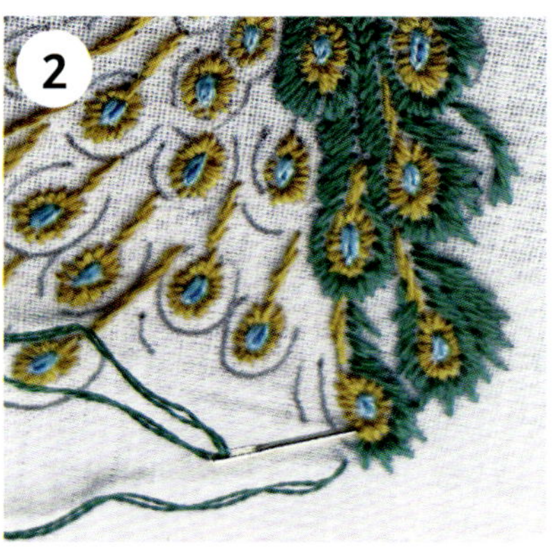

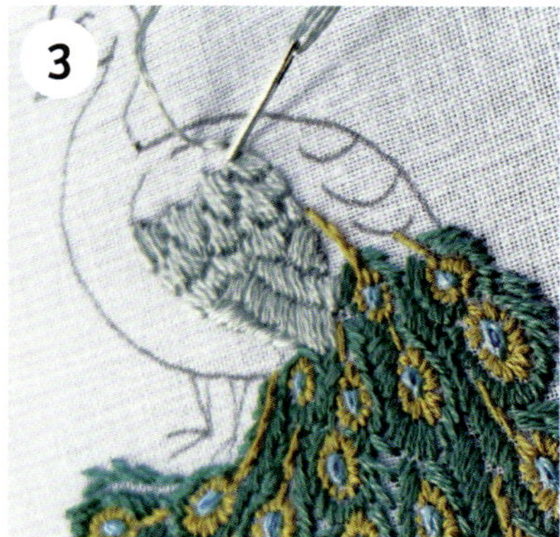

Motif 13:
Rabbit

This cute bunny would make a lovely design for an Easter decoration.

Thread colours

- 436 cappuccino
- 642 stone
- 3046 beige
- B5200 white
- 310 black
- 918 chestnut
- 353 blush

Use two strands of thread throughout, unless otherwise stated.

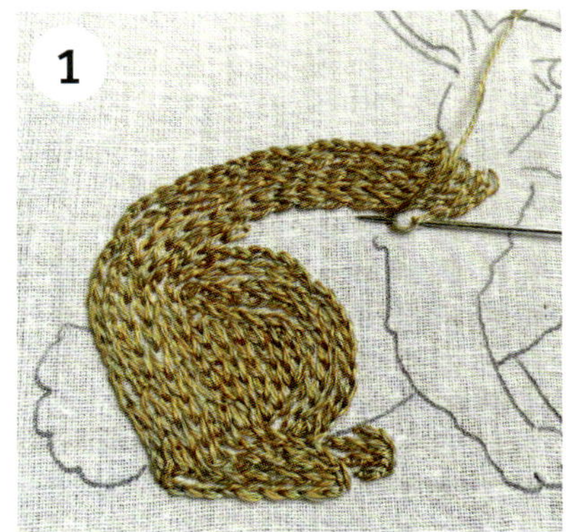

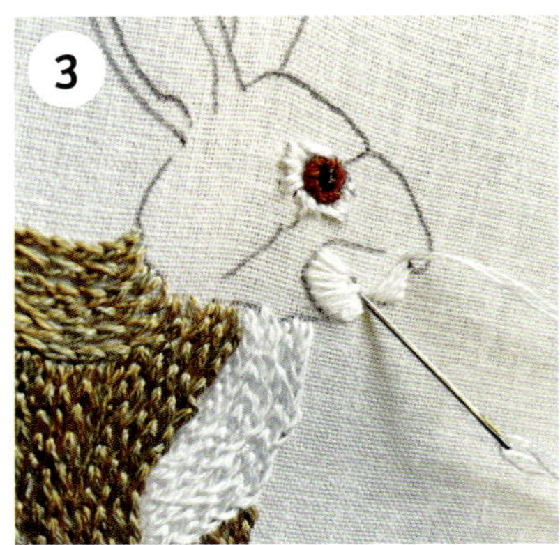

1. Thread the needle with one strand of 436 and one of 642 and fill in the main part of the body and the legs with chain stitch filling, working the rows in the direction of the fur's growth.
2. For the tummy section between the front and back leg and the front of the face around the muzzle, change to two strands of 3046. Still using chain stitch, fill in the chest and tail with B5200.
3. Start the head by filling in the eye with satin stitch: the centre with 310 and the iris with 918, then fill in the surrounding area and the muzzle with B5200.
4. Fill in the centre of the ear and the tip of the nose with 353 and split stitch filling. Complete the ears with one strand each of 436 and 642 and satin stitch, then use this combination for the back part of the head, using chain stitch. Fill in the front of the face around the muzzle with two strands of
5. As a final touch, add a few whiskers freehand with a few straight stitches and a single strand of 642.

Motif 14: Cat

Here's one for cat lovers: a friendly puss with a cheeky smile, with a sample of the design stitched to resemble a stripy tabby.

Thread colours

- 436 cappuccino
- 783 mustard
- 642 stone
- 869 cocoa
- 605 shell pink
- 907 lime
- 645 dark grey

Use two strands of thread throughout, unless otherwise stated.

1. Use 436 and backstitch to outline the whole shape of the cat. Try to keep the stitches an equal length, but you may need to adjust them as you go around corners. Don't forget to backstitch the lines between the legs.
2. Fill in the stripes and other markings in satin stitch for the wider areas or stem stitch where the width is narrow, using 436, 783, 642 and 869.
3. Using satin stitch, fill in the nose using 605 and the eyes using 907 and 645. With backstitch, embroider the whiskers with a single strand of 645.

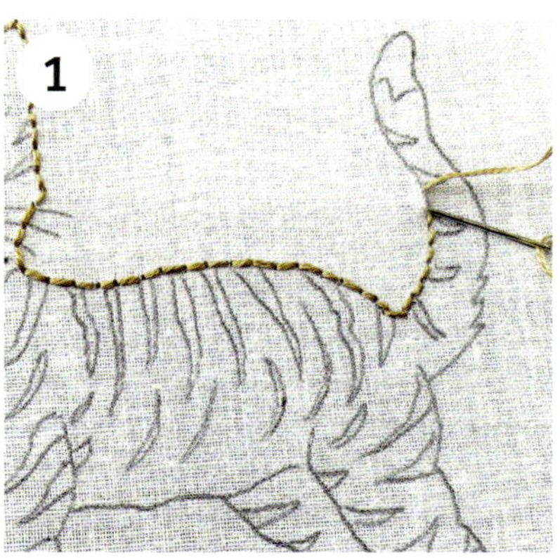

Creative ideas

Change your cat to a ginger tom or tortoiseshell by choosing appropriate thread colours for the stripes, change the markings to patches, or simply fill in the whole shape for a solid-coloured cat. Frame your finished embroidery for a cat-loving friend.

Motif 15:
Dog

Who can resist this little puppy, with its patches just waiting to be filled with thread, bringing the picture to life?

Thread colours

- 310 black
- 869 cocoa
- 3046 beige
- 436 cappuccino
- 840 sepia
- B5200 white

Use two strands of thread throughout.

1. Using satin stitch, fill in the nose and the pupils of the eyes in 310. Complete the eyes with 869.
2. Change to 3046 and split stitch filling, and fill in the eye patch, then the patch on the left shoulder and the right hind leg. Use 436 for the patches on the ears, the chin, the right shoulder and left front leg.
3. Use 840 to fill in the remaining patches and the tail, then follow all the exposed outlines with split stitch.
4. Using B5200, make a single small stitch on the pupil of each eye and the top of the nose.

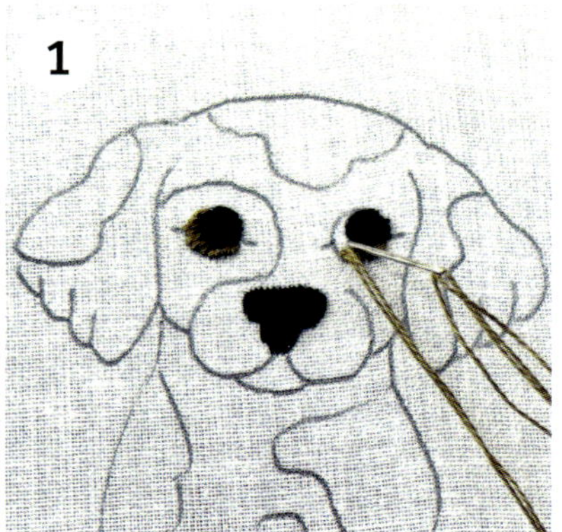

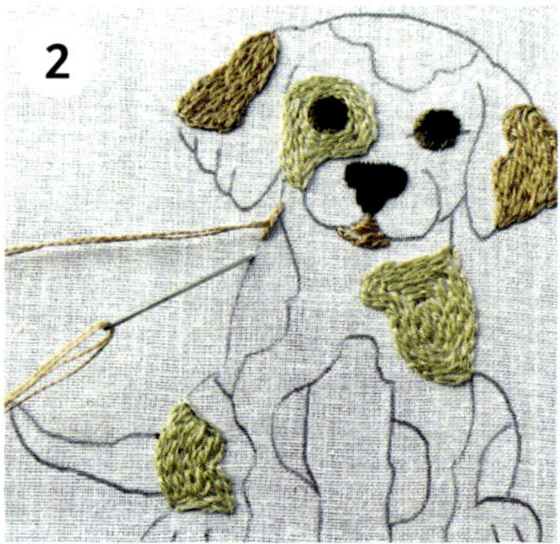

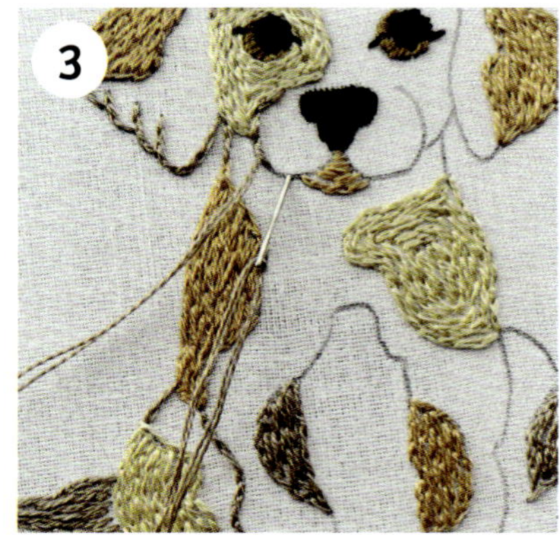

Creative ideas

You can, of course, customize this motif – perhaps draw the patches in different positions and change the thread colour palette. Make it your own!

Motif 16:
Hummingbird

Hummingbirds are colourful creatures, so you will need a good range of coloured threads for this one – whether you follow scheme used here or create your own palette!

Thread colours

- 907 lime
- 943 pine green
- 3846 aqua
- 800 sky blue
- 3609 heliotrope
- 340 lavender
- 995 turquoise
- B5200 white
- 310 black
- 891 watermelon
- 703 shamrock
- 608 flame
- 741 tangerine

Use two strands of thread throughout.

1. Use 907 and satin stitch to fill in the crescent shape just below the wing. Then, combining one strand of 907 and one strand of 943, fill in the fluted shape at the base of the wing. Fill in the next shape with 943 and the following with 3846.
2. For the long wing feathers, work satin stitch across each one, starting with 800 for the shorter feathers and at the base of the longer ones, a combination of 800 and 3609 in the centre of the feathers, and 3609 at the tips.
3. Now move on to the body and continuing with satin stitch, fill in the central wavy stripe in 3846 and the belly in 340. Fill in the round shape at the base of the tail with 943 and the top of the body with 907.
4. Fill in the neck stripe with 995 in satin stitch, then the lower half of the head with 340 and split stitch filling. Fill the eye with B5200 and satin stitch. Fill the upper part of the head with long-and-short stitch, using 3846 and 995.
5. To finish the bird, embroider the remaining feathers using 800 and 3609, as before, and use a French knot with 310 for the centre of the eye. For the beak, use 891 in satin stitch.
6. For the background, use 703 and stem stitch for the flower stem, then the same colour in satin stitch for the leaves. For the flower centre, use 907 and work satin stitches from the edge of the circle to the centre. For the petals, use long-and-short stitch with 608 at the base of each petal and 741 for the tips. For the scattering of little dots use 907, as here, or any colour you like.

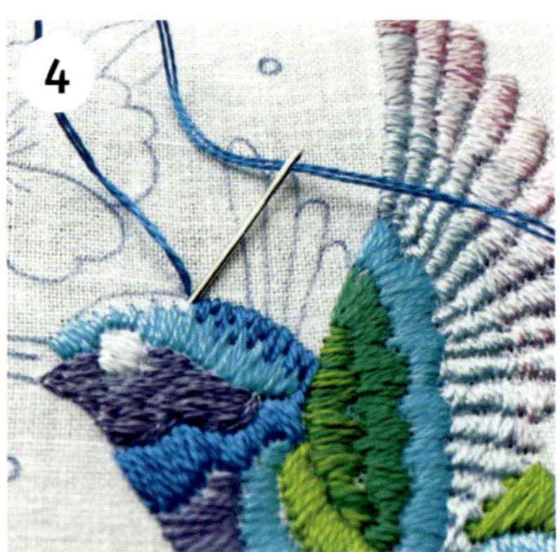

Notes on technique

As a general rule, when there are numerous shapes to be filled, it is a good idea to start in the centre of the design and work outwards.

Motif 17:
Horse

Focusing on the head and bridle, an outlining technique is used for speed and ease, making this an ideal motif for a novice.

Thread colours

- 645 dark grey
- 310 black
- 783 mustard
- 927 grey
- 869 cocoa

Use two strands of thread throughout, unless otherwise stated.

Notes on technique

If you have the time and patience, you can fill in the whole design with a rich filling stitch such as split stitch filling or long-and-short stitch.

1. Start by embroidering the bridle with padded satin stitch: using two strands of 645, sew lines of running stitch down the centre of each strap, then go over each one with satin stitch. Fill in the nostril and the pupil of the eye using 310 and satin stitch.
2. For the mane, use 783 and fill each strand with satin stitch, working the stitches at a slant. Stitch the small rings and buckle using 927 and satin stitch.
3. Finally, work the outline in backstitch, using three strands of 869, and finish the eye in the same colour using satin stitch.

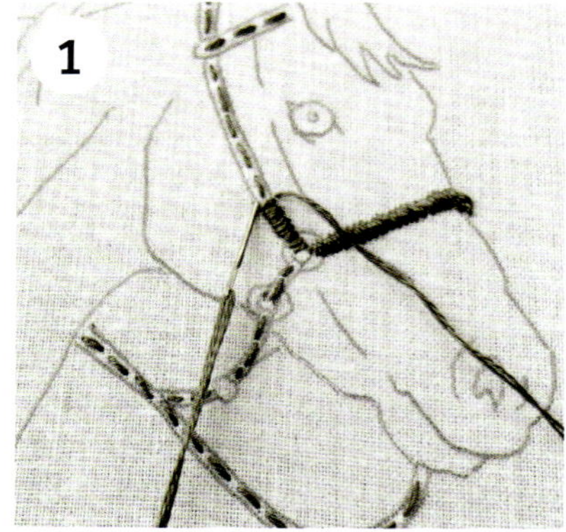

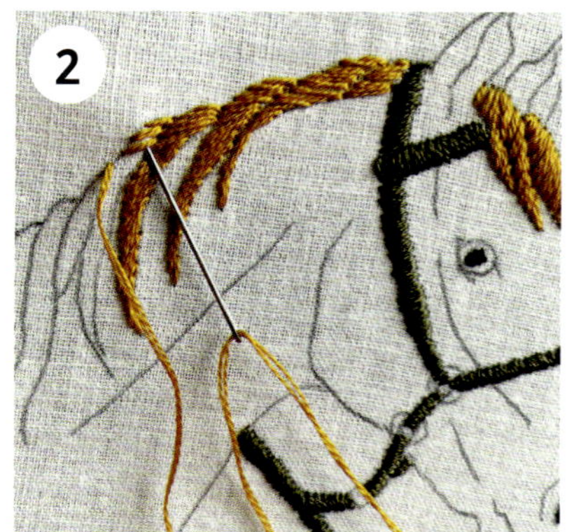

Motif 18:
Birds and Bees

On a dainty scale, these little birds and insects inhabit a decorative motif that can be adapted to various colour schemes. Its square format makes it perfect for a greetings card or as a central panel on a cushion.

Thread colours

- 703 shamrock
- 335 pomegranate
- 927 grey
- 800 sky blue
- 645 dark grey
- 444 yellow
- 746 ivory

Use two strands of thread throughout, unless otherwise stated.

1. Starting with the structure of stems and leaves in 703, use stem stitch for the stems and satin stitch for the leaves, then use satin stitch for all the berries in 335.
2. Fill in the head and body of each bird with split stitch filling and 927, then fill in the wings, section by section, in 800 sky blue and satin stitch.
3. Starting at the head end of each bee, use 645 and 444 to fill in alternate sections of the body in satin stitch. While you have these colours in your needle, fill in the birds' beaks with 444 and satin stitch, and add a French knot in 645 for each eye.
4. Use 335 and split stitch for the birds' legs and feet. Fill in the bees' wings with satin stitch, using 746, then use a single strand of 645 for the legs and antennae.

Notes on technique

Planning the order in which to stitch the elements of the design is important. For example, the birds' feet overlap the stems, so embroider the stems first.

Motif 19:
Camel

This camel is wearing a saddle, giving some scope for using attractive colours and patterns in your embroidery.

Thread colours

- 436 cappuccino
- 3046 beige
- 347 russet
- 444 yellow
- 702 fern
- 642 stone

Use two strands of thread throughout.

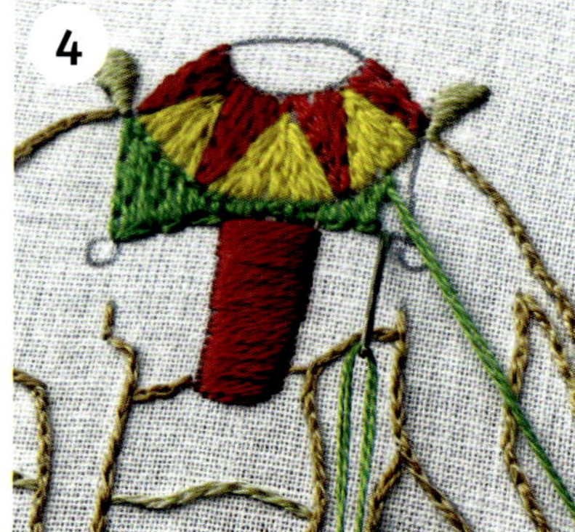

1. Use 436 and split stitch to outline the camel, then switch to 3046 to split stitch the horizon line.
2. Still using 3046, fill in the two pommels on the saddle with satin stitch. Using 347, fill in the bridle and girth with satin stitch.
3. Still using 347, fill in four of the triangular shapes on the saddle with split stitch filling; now fill in the other three using 444.
4. Fill in the rest of the saddle with split stitch filling using 702. Fill in the three small tassels using 444 and satin stitch, and finally embroider the eye using 642 and straight stitches.

Creative ideas

Repeat the motif on a long strip of fabric, creating a camel train. You can link the camels with looped lines embroidered in an outline stitch such as backstitch or split stitch, and customize each saddle with different colours and patterns. This would make an attractive border for a curtain or similar item.

Motif 20:
Kangaroos

This motif lends itself very well to an outlining treatment, making it quick to stitch – but you could just as easily fill in the shapes with satin stitch or split stitch filling if you prefer.

Thread colours

- 436 cappuccino
- 3046 beige
- 840 sepia
- 645 dark grey
- 988 sage

Use two strands of thread throughout.

1. Using 436 and split stitch, follow the line through the centre of the adult kangeroo's body and tail and horizontally along the centre of the head.
2. In a similar way, use 3046 along the underside of the tail, the front of the body and the underside of the head, then use 840 for the remaining outlines on the kangaroo. Now use 840 and the same split stitch on the tree trunk, then the fence and the horizon line.
3. Using satin stitch, fill in the eyes and noses using 645 and the leaves on the tree using 988.

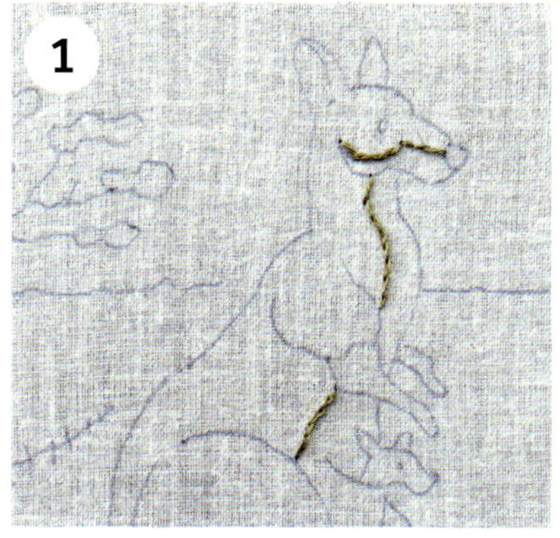

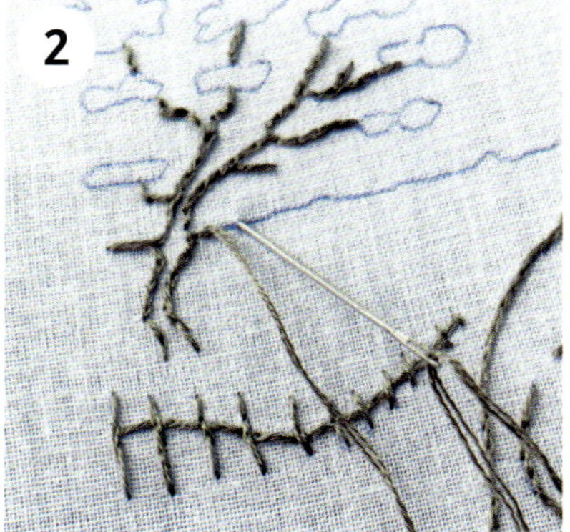

Creative ideas

Use this motif to make a card for a new baby or for friends who may be emigrating to Australia. You could also use it alongside other animal motifs to make a rag book for a baby or toddler.

Motif 21:
Mushrooms

Whether they are mushrooms or toadstools – there is no scientific difference – these forest fungi provide a haven for a solitary snail.

Thread colours

- 746 ivory
- 988 sage
- B5200 white
- 666 red
- 642 stone
- 840 sepia
- 3046 beige
- 436 cappuccino
- 783 mustard

Use two strands of thread throughout, unless otherwise stated.

1. Fill in the stalks with split stitch filling and 746, with the lines of stitches running vertically. Use split stitch for the outlines of the little mounds at the base of the stalks, using 988.
2. Fill in the spots in B5200 and satin stitch, then fill in the caps of the three smaller mushrooms in 666, first outlining it in split stitch and then using split stitch filling.
3. For the gills seen in one of the small mushrooms, use one strand each of 642 and 746 and satin stitch, with the stitches radiating out from the top of the stalk. For the gills hanging below the cap of the small mushroom, work short lines of split stitch using two strands of 642.
4. For the large mushroom, follow the lines of the gills with split stitch and three strands of 840, and outline the top of the stalk, then fill in the spaces in between using the 642 and 746 combination. Fill in the cap using split stitch filling and 3046.
5. For the snail, use satin stitch with 436 for the body and 783 for the shell. Add definition to the shell by outlining the spiral with a single strand of 840 in backstitch, and also use this for the antennae.

Creative ideas

Repeat the motif on a long strip of fabric, creating a row of mushrooms. You can link the mushrooms with looped lines embroidered in an outline stitch such as backstitch or split stitch, and customize each cap with different colours and spots. This would then make an attractive border for a curtain or similar item.

Motif 22: Cactus

A cactus makes a great little potted plant that is easy to care for – and this stitched version is easy to work. You can choose your own colours for the pretty cactus flower.

Thread colours

- 444 yellow
- 741 tangerine
- 840 sepia
- 783 mustard
- 702 fern

Use two strands of thread throughout, unless otherwise stated.

1. Starting with the flower and satin stitch, use 444 to fill in the flower centre and 741 for the petals.
2. Still using satin stitch, fill in the small area of soil in the pot with 840. Fill in the pot using split stitch filling in 783. You can start by outlining the pot before filling in the rest of the shape. For the horizontal line on either side of the pot, use 840 in split stitch.
3. For the catcus itself, using 702 and chain stitch, embroider along the outline and the long lines on the cactus, then add the little spikes with split stitch in a single strand.

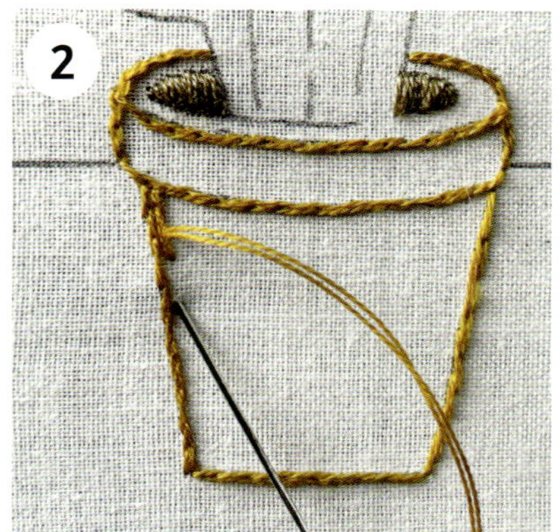

Creative ideas

This motif could be repeated multiple times as an all-over pattern on a garment, bag or cushion cover, or in a line along the hem of a curtain. If you decide to do this, you may wish to omit the horizontal line; you could also use different colours for each cactus flower.

Motif 23:
Thistle

The national flower of Scotland, thistles have leaves with sharp prickles and flower heads comprising a ball of spiny bracts topped with a cluster of florets.

Thread colours

- 907 lime
- 988 sage
- 3607 red-violet
- 3609 heliotrope

Use two strands of thread throughout.

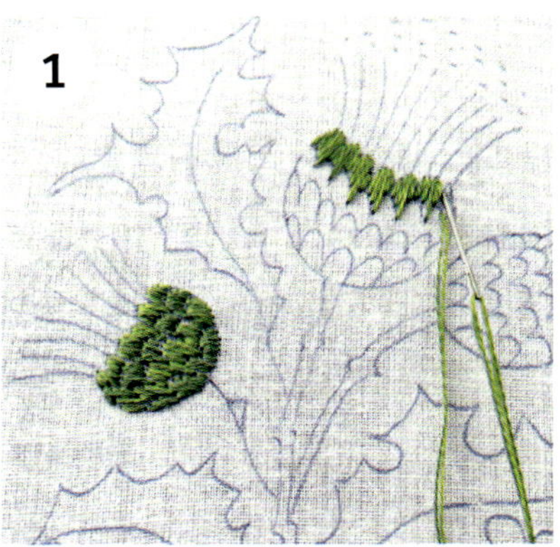

1. Thread your needle with one strand of 907 and one of 988 and fill in the top row of bracts at the base of the thistle flower with satin stitch, working the stitches across the row. For the next row, use two strands of 988, then the row below go back to the 907 and 988 combination, working towards the base and alternating the colours in the rows.
2. Moving on to the stems and leaves, with 907, fill in the stems with satin stitch and the leaf veins with raised stem stitch.
3. Now, with 988, fill in the leaves. On the narrow parts, use satin stitch; on the wider areas, use long-and-short stitch.
4. For the petals, with a combination of 3607 and 3609 in the needle, stitch along the lines that form the top of the flowers with split stitch. This forms the foundation. Build upon this by adding a number of straight stitches – like an open satin stitch – the full height of the flower. Finish with a sprinkling of French knots above.

Notes on technique

For the flower heads, the layer of long straight stitches may not be practical for something like a cushion or quilt, where the stitches may get snagged.

Motif 24:
Dandelion

Considered a weed, this ubiquitous member of the daisy family has bright yellow flowers followed by globe-like seed heads with downy tufts, known colloquially as clocks. The name 'dandelion' derives from the French word for lion's teeth and the flowers, leaves and roots are all edible.

Thread colours

- 907 lime
- 702 fern
- 307 buttermilk
- 444 yellow
- 746 ivory
- B5200 white

Use two strands of thread throughout.

1. With 907, embroider the stems and leaf veins, using satin stitch for the thicker lines and stem stitch for the finer ones.
2. Change to 702 and satin stitch for the leaves and the bracts below the flower and the bud, as well as the bud itself. Fill in the centre of the flower, still using satin stitch, with 307 and the outer petals with 444.
3. For the seed heads, thread the needle with one strand each of 746 and B5200 and fill in the centre circle of each with satin stitch, working the stitches towards the centre point.
4. Now work straight stitches, bringing the needle up on the circle of dots and down at the circumference of the centre circle. Work another round of shorter stitches in between the first round, then top each stitch with a French knot and work more French knots freehand.

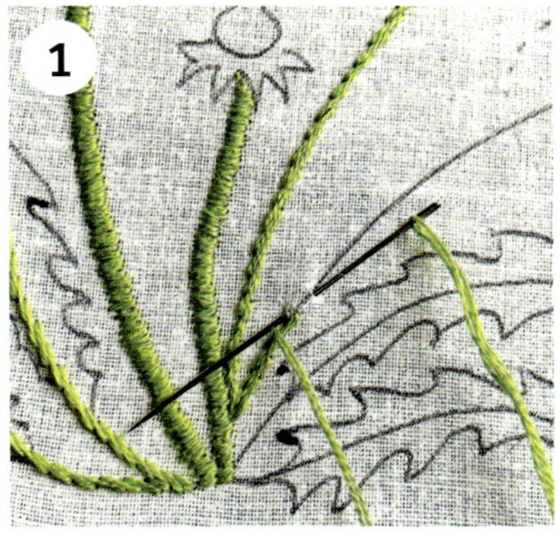

Notes on technique

Because the seed heads are worked with open stitches, the fabric will show through, so take care when drawing on the fabric to avoid creating any marks that might not be covered with thread. A ballpoint pen has been used here to mark out the design, but you may prefer to use an erasable marker.

Motif 25: Acorns

Acorns are the fruits of the oak tree, consisting of a hard-shelled nut held in a little cap called a cupule.

Thread colours

- 642 stone
- 907 lime
- 988 sage
- 783 mustard
- 436 cappuccino

Use two strands of thread throughout, unless otherwise stated.

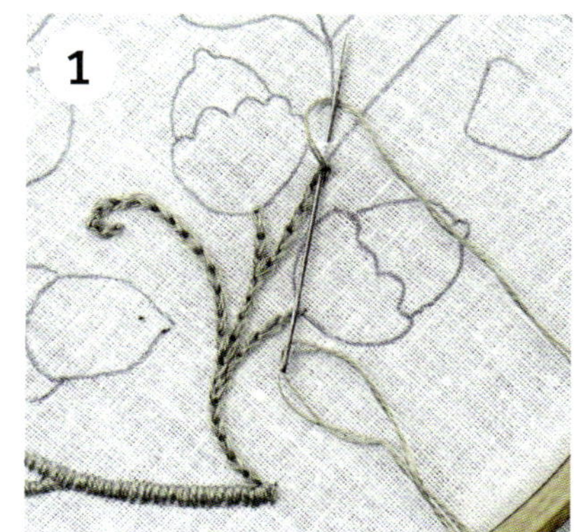

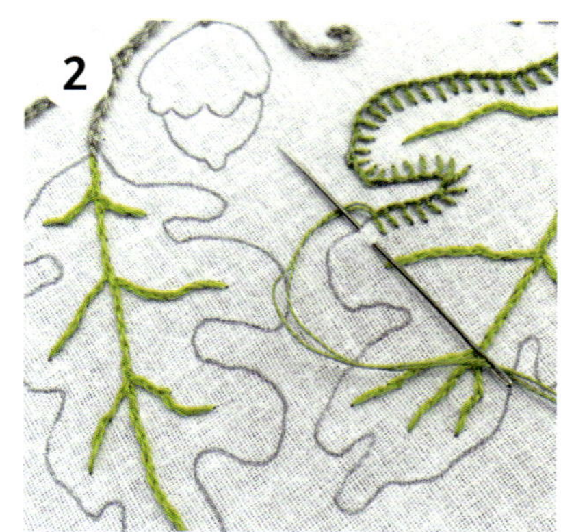

1. Using 642, fill in the thicker stem in satin stitch, then use chain stitch for the thinner stems.
2. Use 907 and split stitch for the leaf veins. Change to 988 and outline the smallest leaf in split stitch and the larger ones in blanket stitch.
3. For the acorns, thread the needle with one strand of 783 and one strand of 436. Using satin stitch, fill in the two smaller nuts. For the largest of the three, change to long-and-short stitch.
4. For the cupule, first use one strand of 436 to outline the shape with backstitch, then fill in the shape with satin stitch.
5. Now thread the needle with one strand of 436 and one strand of 642 and fill the shape with French knots.

Notes on technique

When working both chain stitch and French knots, the thread tends to become twisted. To prevent this, from time to time drop the needle and let it dangle, allowing the thread to untwist before continuing.

Motif 26:
Water Lilies

Two pretty water lilies and their green lily pads sit on the surface of a pond, depicted by a few watery swirls.

Thread colours

- 956 rose pink
- 894 candy pink
- 907 lime
- 891 watermelon
- 742 apricot
- B5200 white
- 703 shamrock
- 701 emerald
- 800 sky blue

Use two strands of thread throughout, unless otherwise stated.

1. Starting from the centre and working outwards, fill in the flower petals with satin stitch, working the stitches across the width of each petal. Use 956 for one lily and 894 for the other lily and flower bud. Fill in the stem between the lily and bud in 907, still using satin stitch.
2. Outline the inner petals of each flower in split stitch, using 891 for the darker flower and 956 for the lighter one. Now add stamens in 742, making a series of straight stitches and adding French knots. Add a few straight stitches in 894 and B5200 to outline the tips of the outer petals.
3. Fill in the leaves using 907 and 703 and split stitch filling, with the lines of stitching following the contours of the shapes.
4. Add lines of split stitch to denote leaf veins, using 701. Finally, embroider the ripples in stem stitch using 800.

Creative ideas

Flowers of all kinds are the most popular subjects for embroidery. These lilies would make a lovely greetings card.

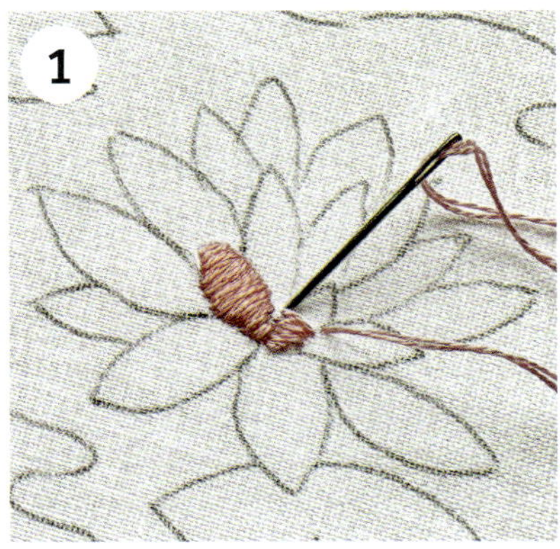

Motif 27:
Apple Blossom

Apple blossoms herald the arrival of spring, which for many people symbolizes rebirth, regeneration and the wonders of nature. These delicate flowers and buds also provide a beautiful subject for embroidery.

Thread colours

- 869 cocoa
- 436 cappuccino
- 702 fern
- 335 pomegranate
- B5200 white
- 605 shell pink
- 444 yellow

Use two strands of thread throughout.

1. Start by embroidering the branch and stems. For the thicker parts, combine one strand each of 869 and 436 in your needle and, working across the shapes, fill them in with satin stitch. For the thinner stems, use 702 and stem stitch.
2. Still using 702, fill in the tiny leaves and the sepals at the base of each bud, using satin stitch. For the buds, use 335 and satin stich.
3. Fill in the flower petals using B5200 and straight stitches: bring the needle up through the fabric just inside the outline of the petal and down close to the centre.
4. Cover the outline of the petals by working split stitch around their perimeter, covering the exposed drawn lines with 605. You can also use this thread colour to work a few straight stitches on top of the white petals, radiating from the flower centre. Finish with a ring of French knots around the centre of each open blossom, using 444.

Notes on technique

When using split stitch to outline intricate shapes like these flower petals, keep the stitches small so they can follow curves and contours.

Motif 28: Artichoke

Artichokes are among the most decorative of vegetables, with their petals forming an attractive rosette.

Thread colours

- 16 celery
- 703 shamrock
- 988 sage
- B5200 white
- 210 lilac
- 553 grape

Use two strands of thread throughout.

1. Using 16, fill in the cut base and the leaves on the stem with satin stitch, working the stitches across the shapes, then work three close rows of split stitch vertically down the left-hand side of the stem.
2. Thread the needle with one strand each of 16 and 703 and work three more rows. Now, still working in vertical rows, fill in the rest of the stalk with 703.
3. Start filling in the petals from the base, working upwards. Fill in the two narrowest petals using satin stitch and 988.
4. Now change to long-and-short stitch: for the next rows of petals in the lower section, start each one with one strand each of 988 and 703, then 703 alone, then 703 combined with 16, then 16 alone. Use B5200 for the edges of the petals.
5. For the upper petals, start to include the purple shades, 210 and 553, combining them with 703, 16 and B5200. For the petals above the final white stitches, use 210 and 553 in satin stitch.

Notes on technique

Long-and-short stitch can be a bit tricky to master, but it's worth persevering as it can create some very attractive effects, especially when you also combine more than one colour of thread in the needle.

Motif 29:
Rose

In art, literature and poetry, this popular flower has been celebrated as a symbol of devotion and beauty. Scottish poet Robert Burns famously said, "My love is like a red, red rose."

Thread colours

- 347 russet
- 891 watermelon
- 666 red
- 703 shamrock
- 702 fern
- 436 cappuccino

Use two strands of thread throughout.

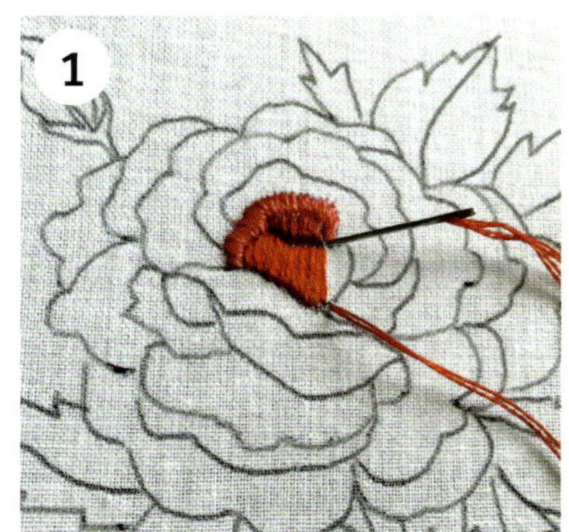

1. Start in the centre and work outwards. Begin with 347 and the smallest shape, filling it in with satin stitch, then fill in the little shape above with 891 and the one below with 666.
2. Continue with these three colours and fill in the whole flower, petal by petal, using the bright shade for most of the petals, changing to the light shade for some of the petal edges and using the dark shade for contrast. You can use your judgement for this, or refer to the picture of the finished embroidery.
3. Embroider the leaf veins in overcast stitch, using 703, then fill in the rest of the leaves with satin stitch in 702. For the stem, use satin stitch and 436, and for the thorns and the base of the stem use 703, again using satin stitch.

Creative ideas

Roses come in lots of beautiful colours. Whatever colour you choose, try to use several shades for best effect.

Motif 30:
Pumpkins

There are more than 150 different varieties of these hard-skinned fruit, a popular Halloween decoration and a symbol of the autumn harvest.

Thread colours

- 988 sage
- 703 shamrock
- 740 orange
- 741 tangerine

Use two strands of thread throughout.

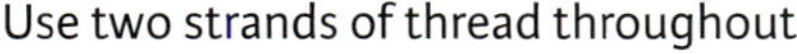

1. Use 988 and 703 with satin stitch for the stems and leaves. Where the stems taper to a thin line, transition from satin stitch to stem stitch.
2. Using split stitch filling, fill in the pumpkins one segment at a time. Starting at the left of the larger pumpkin, use 740 for the left half of the segment and 741 for the right-hand side. Move on to the next segment and repeat.
3. Now, for the middle segment, use 740 on either side and 741 for the centre. Continue with the two right-hand segments, reversing the colours.
4. Fill in the small back segments using 740, then fill in the smaller pumpkin using a similar method.

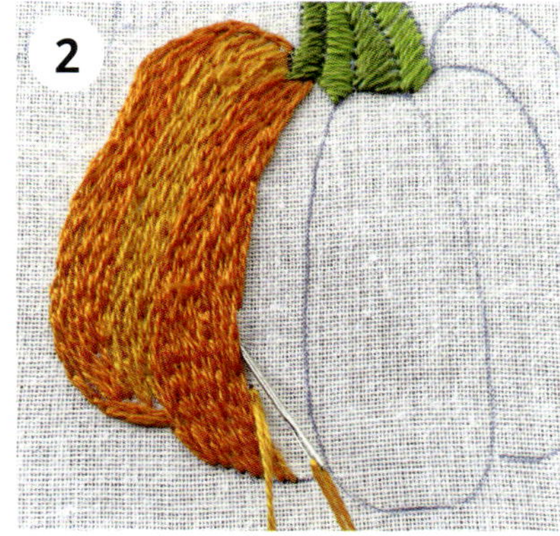

Notes on technique

There are some tight twists in the pumpkin stems, so work the stem stitch with very short stitches to accommodate the curves.

Motif 31:
Grapes

Grapes grow on deciduous woody vines and both the fruit – which are actually berries – and the leaves are edible. In this example, raised stem stitch and overcast stitch create raised lines, adding texture, while split stitch shading creates an attractive blended effect.

Thread colours

- 907 lime
- 988 sage
- 436 cappuccino
- 16 celery
- 208 violet
- 553 grape
- 210 lilac
- B5200 white

Use two strands of thread throughout.

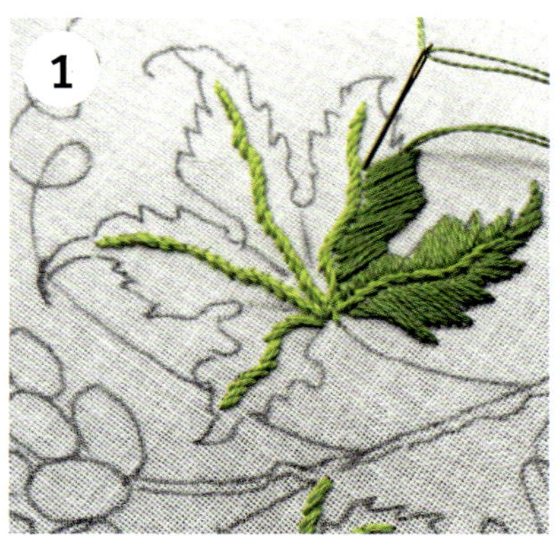

1. Start with the leaf veins, stitching them in raised stem stitch using 907, then fill in the leaves with satin stitch, using 988.
2. Embroider the main stem in satin stitch, using 436. For the tendrils, use overcast stitch and 907, changing to 16 for the smallest tendril, near the base of the main stem.
3. For the grapes, use split stitch shading and the three shades of purple: 208, 553 and 210. Working for the darkest to lightest shades and working inwards, outline each grape with 208, switch to 553 and finish with 210. Add a few single-stitch highlights in B5200.

Notes on technique

You may wish to simplify things – and save on thread – by choosing more straightforward stitches. You could use regular stem stitch for the leaf veins, backstitch or split stitch for the tendrils, and satin stitch for the grapes.

Motif 32: Strawberries

A strawberry isn't actually a berry but a cluster of lots of individual fruits. It's the little seeds that are the fruits. Of course, this makes no difference to your embroidery: just choose a juicy red thread and start stitching!

Thread colours

- 703 shamrock
- 907 lime
- 746 ivory
- 16 celery
- 307 buttermilk
- 666 red
- 444 yellow

Use two strands of thread throughout.

1. Create a framework for your embroidery by stitching the stems and leaf veins in overcast stitch, using 703. With the same colour, fill in the calyxes at the base of the strawberries with satin stitch. Use 907, a lighter shade of green, to complete the leaves in satin stitch.
2. For the flowers, embroider the petals in satin stitch using 746, with the stitch direction fanning outwards from the centre. Layer and overlap the stitches quite thickly for a rich, padded effect. Fill in the centres with French knots, using one strand of 16 and one strand of 307.
3. Fill in the strawberries with split stitch filling and 666. Using 444, add seeds to the strawberries with small detached chain stitches.

Notes on technique

When transferring the design onto fabric, there is no need to include the seeds on the strawberries as these marks would be covered up. Once you have embroidered the strawberries with red thread, you can add the seeds on top, referring to the outline motif to position them.

Motif 33:
Lemon and Lime

Juicy and zesty, lemons and limes have lovely bright colours, so this pair makes an eye-catching motif.

Thread colours

- B5200 white
- 444 yellow
- 907 lime
- 701 emerald
- 307 buttermilk
- 16 celery

Use two strands of thread throughout.

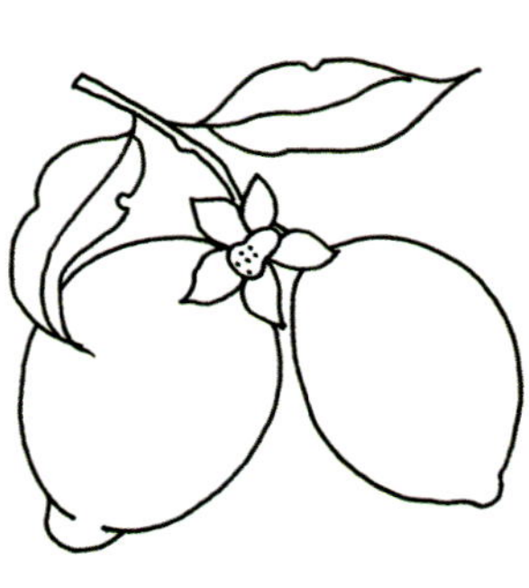

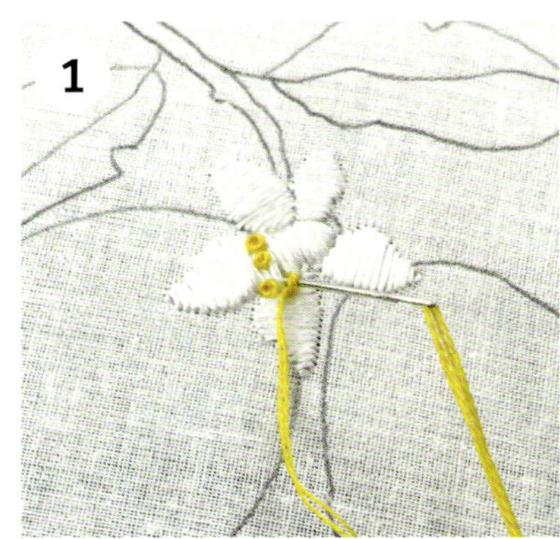

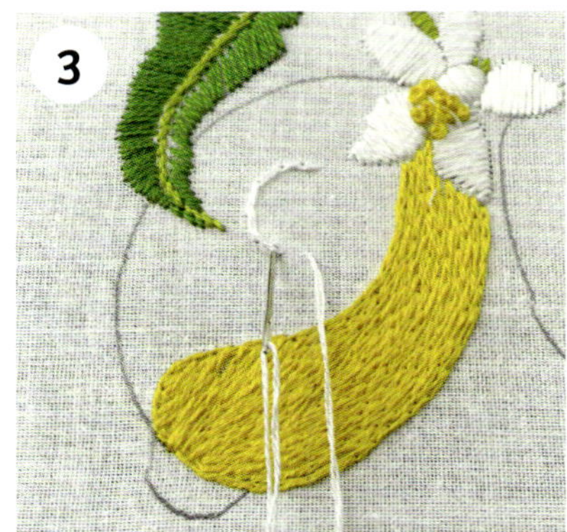

1. Fill in each section of the flower with satin stitch in B5200, then add a cluster of French knots in 444.
2. Fill in the stem with satin stitch and 907, then use the same colour for the leaf veins, using stem stitch. Fill in the leaves with satin stitch and 701.
3. Fill in about one third of the lemon with 444 and split stitch filling. Now, with a row of B5200, create an outline for a patch of highlight with split stitches. Next, surround it with a few rows of split stitches using one strand of B5200 and one of 307, then fill in the remaining lemon, including the little bump at the base, with 307.
4. Treat the lime in a similar way, using 907, B5200 and 16.

Notes on technique

Three colours are used to fill in each fruit. This involves dividing them into sections, which you can do 'by eye' or by marking out the sections with a marker pen.

Motif 34: Beetroot

This nutritious root vegetable – known as beetroot in the UK and beet in North America – comes in various shades of reddish purple. There are even striped varieties!

Thread colours

- B5200 white
- 891 watermelon
- 347 russet
- 702 fern

Use two strands of thread throughout, unless otherwise stated.

1. Fill in the highlight using satin stitch and B5200, then outline it with 891 and split stitch. Fill in the rest of the beetroot in split stitch filling, using 347, starting with the outline and working inwards in a spiral.
2. Use one strand of 891 and split stitch for the fine roots, then a combination of split stitch and stem stitch and two strands for the stems and leaf veins.
3. Fill in the leaves with 702. Use satin stitch and, where the areas to be filled are quite wide, divide the area into two sections, working each with a separate row of stitches.

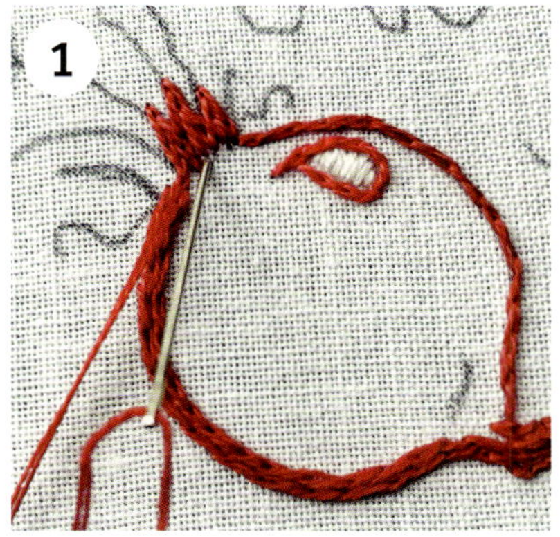

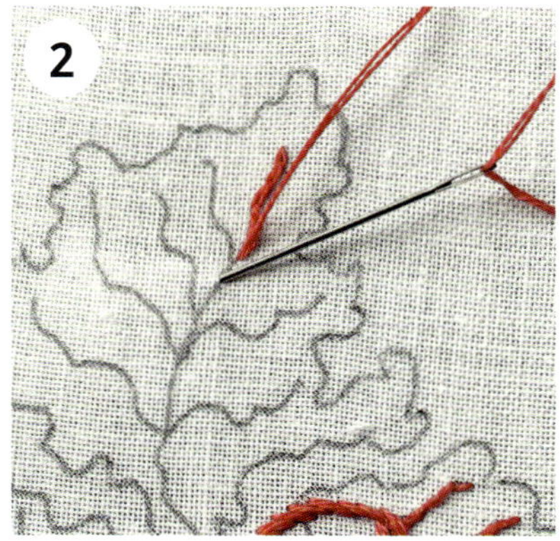

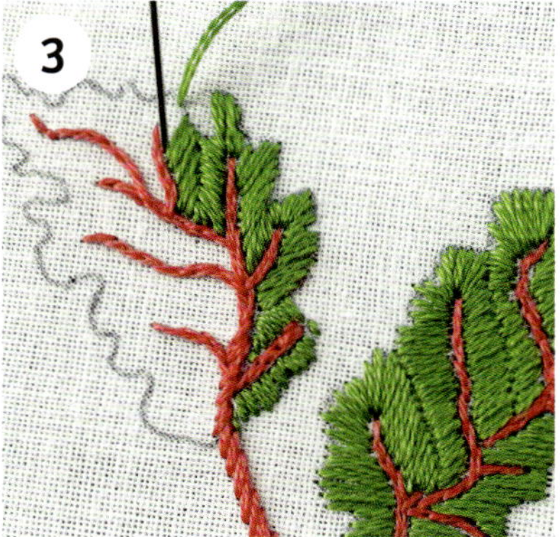

Notes on technique

Satin stitch is best confined to small or narrow areas. If the area to be filled is too wide, you can divide it into smaller or narrower shapes, thereby keeping the stitches nice and short and less liable to snag.

Motif 35:
Corn

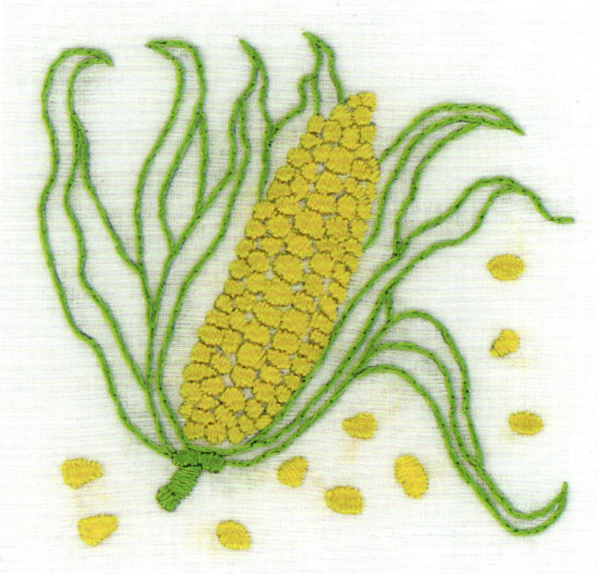

The origins of corn on the cob can be traced back at least 8,000 years to Mexico. The kernels are not always yellow – there are varieties that are white, pink, red, blue and black. The outer leaves are called husks.

Thread colours

- 444 yellow
- 703 shamrock
- 907 lime

Use two strands of thread throughout.

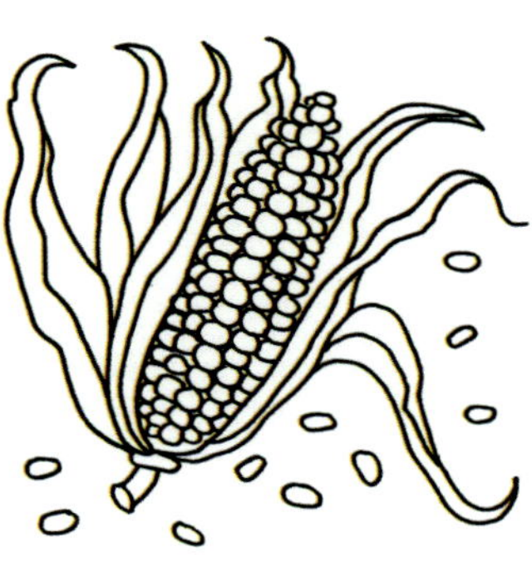

1. Using 444, embroider each kernel individually, using padded satin stitch. Start by stitching two straight stitches lengthways inside each small shape, then fill in the shape with satin stitch, with the stitches going in the other direction.
2. Thread the needle with one strand of 703 and one of 907. Fill in the stalk with satin stitch.
3. Now follow the outlines of the leaves – or, rather, the husks – with split stitch, using the 703 and 907 combination. You can vary the length of the stitches, making them longer on the straight parts of the leaves and shorter where the leaves bend.

Creative ideas

This motif could be repeated multiple times as an all-over pattern on a kitchen curtain or a shopping bag. You could pair it with the Cactus from page 47 for a Mexican-themed project.

Motif 36:
Figs

Still attached to the branch, one of these figs has been cut open to reveal the fleshy interior.

Thread colours

- 436 cappuccino
- 16 celery
- 988 sage
- 891 watermelon
- 307 buttermilk
- 208 violet
- 746 ivory
- 3607 red-violet

Use two strands of thread throughout.

1. Start with the main branch, filling it with 436 and satin stitch. For the smaller stems and cut base of the branch, use 16 in satin stitch, then use the same colour for the leaf veins with overcast stitch. Now outline the leaves using 988 and split stitch.
2. For the cut fig, use split stitch again to embroider the wiggly lines on the inside of the fruit with 891, and add more lines freehand in between, to fill in the gaps.
3. Embroider the seeds using detached chain stitches and 307, then add some more with a scattering of freehand French knots with a double wrap. Now outline this fig with split stitch and 208, then create an inner border of split stitch filling, using 746.
4. Outline the remaining figs with 208 and split stitch, then stitch along the lines with chain stitch, except on the smallest one, where it will be easier and more effective to use split stitch. Fill in the small semicircles at the base of the two larger figs with 307 in satin stitch, then fill in all figs with split stitch filling and 3607.

Notes on technique

When following wiggly lines in split stitch, such as the leaf outlines and the inner part of the fig, keep individual stitches small so they will fit around the many curves and angles.

Motif 37:
Cherries

Cherries are small, round stone fruit that can be sweet or sour. They come in a range of colours, from yellow through shades of red to nearly black, so you can choose your own colour palette.

Thread colours

- 840 sepia
- 907 lime
- 3806 fuchsia
- 605 shell pink
- 307 buttermilk
- 702 fern
- 347 russet
- 666 red
- B5200 white

Use two strands of thread throughout.

1. Using 840, fill in the main stem using satin stitch, then use stem stitch in 907 for the thinner stems and leaf veins.
2. For the blossoms, fill in each petal using long-and-short stitch. Use 3806 for the first row of stitches, radiating out from the centre, and 605 to fill in the remaining part of each petal. Add a few French knots to the flower centres, using 307.
3. Next, fill in the leaves using 702 and satin stitch. Work the stitches diagonally to form the shape of the leaves.
4. Fill in the cherry shapes in split stitch filling, using 347 and 666. Leave a small space on each one, then fill this with a detached chain stitch, using B5200, to create a highlight.

Creative ideas

This motif could be partnered with the Apple Blossom from page 52; they complement each other very well and can be embroidered using similar stitches. Or you could choose other fruits as companion motifs – such as the Grapes (page 56), Strawberries (page 57) and Figs (page 61) – to make a fruity border for a kitchen curtain or a teatime tablecloth.

Motif 38:
Peas

Peas are round seeds that grow in neat rows inside long pods. They are part of the leguminous plant family that not only includes lentils and beans but also peanuts.

Thread colours

- 907 lime
- 645 dark grey
- 703 shamrock
- 701 emerald

Use two strands of thread throughout.

1. Embroider the row of peas in 907 and padded satin stitch, creating nice raised circles.
2. For the area surrounding them inside the pod, use 645 and split stitch filling, then outline the pod using satin stitch and 703.
3. Still using 703, outline the remaining pods with split stitch then fill them in with split stitch filling. For each calyx at the base of the pods, use 701 and satin stitch.
4. Finish by embroidering the stems in overcast stitch, using 703 for the main stem and 907 for the tendrils.

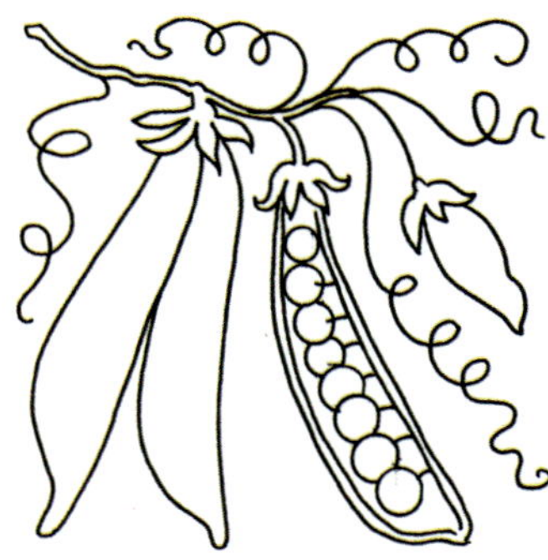

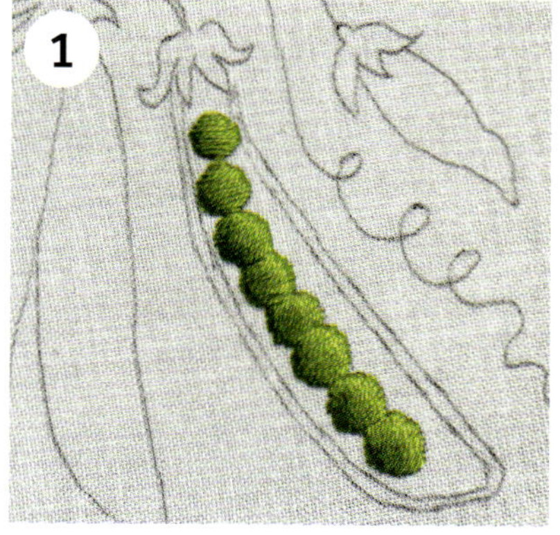

Creative ideas

This is a great design for the kitchen. Use it with the Beetroot (page 59), Figs (page 61) and the Grapes (page 56) for a set of framed pictures or to decorate table linens.

Motif 39:
Carrots

We associate the colour orange with carrots – but these root vegetables, which were first cultivated in Persia over 1,000 years ago, were originally white or pale yellow; red and purple varieties are also grown.

Thread colours

- 741 tangerine
- 907 lime

Use two strands of thread throughout.

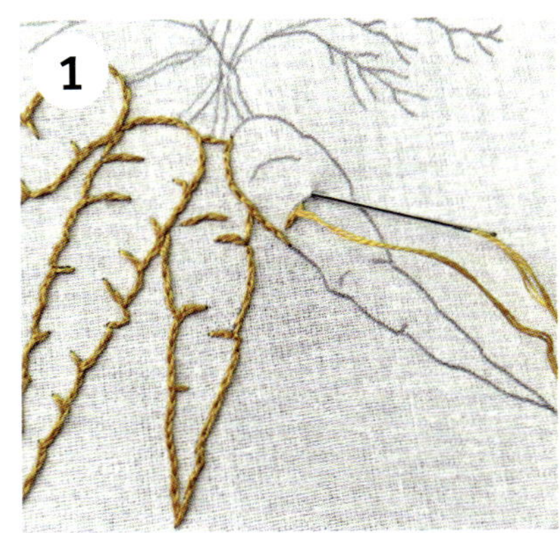

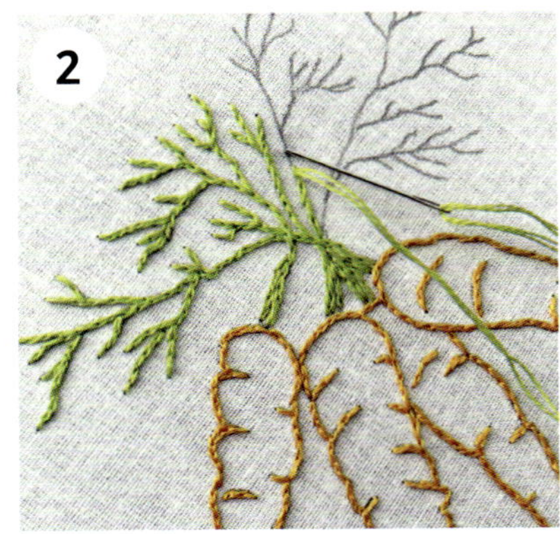

1. Outline the carrots with 741 and split stitch, stitching along each small kink as you come to it.
2. For the fronds, use the same stitch and 907, stitching two rows side by side on the thicker parts.

Notes on technique

Embroidering this motif using only split stitch makes it quick and easy to complete. You could, of course, fill in the carrots with a more solid stitch, if you prefer.

Creative ideas

Decorate a cook's apron with one or more repeats of this motif. It would also look good on the corner of a dinner napkin or along the edge of a tea towel. Combine it with other motifs such as the Lemon and Lime (page 58), Beetroot (page 59), Corn (page 60) and Peas (page 63) for the cover of a recipe file or a grocery bag.

Motif 40:
Poppy

Poppies are very special flowers, not only because they can be used in medicine and cookery but because of their role as a symbol of remembrance, particularly of the First World War.

Thread colours

- 16 celery
- 701 emerald
- 666 red
- 310 black
- 3042 heather

Use two strands of thread throughout, unless otherwise stated.

1. Fill in the centre circle with 16 and satin stitch, working from the outline to the small dot in the centre. Now use 701 to work some straight stitches over it, like spokes on a wheel.
2. Using three strands of 666, work blanket stitch all around the petals' outline.
3. Now change to two strands and work lines of running stitch freehand from the petal edges towards the centre, still using 666.
4. Fill in the main stem and sepals at the base of the buds with 701 and satin stitch, and fill the thinner stems in the same colour in stem stitch. Fill in the flower buds with 666 and satin stitch.
5. With 310, work straight stitches for the stamens, radiating them out from the flower's centre, and with 3042 add a circle of French knots to represent the anthers.

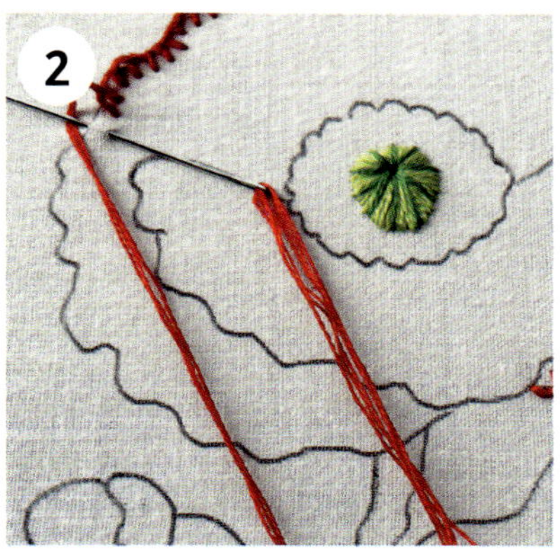

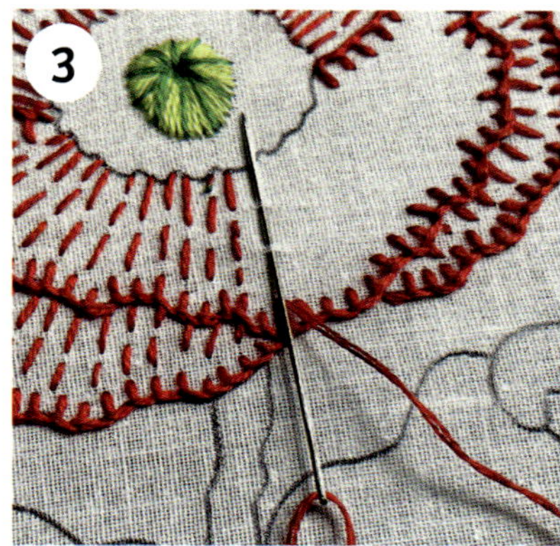

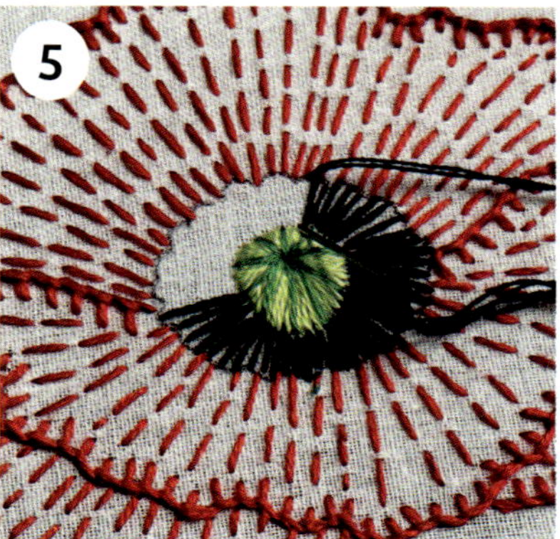

Motif 41:
Seahorse

The seahorse – a member of the genus Hippocampus – is a special kind of fish that swims vertically. This one is sheltering among stalks of kelp.

Thread colours

- 3846 aqua
- 310 black
- 894 candy pink
- 340 lavender
- 741 tangerine
- 608 flame
- 742 apricot
- 3810 sea green

Use two strands of thread throughout.

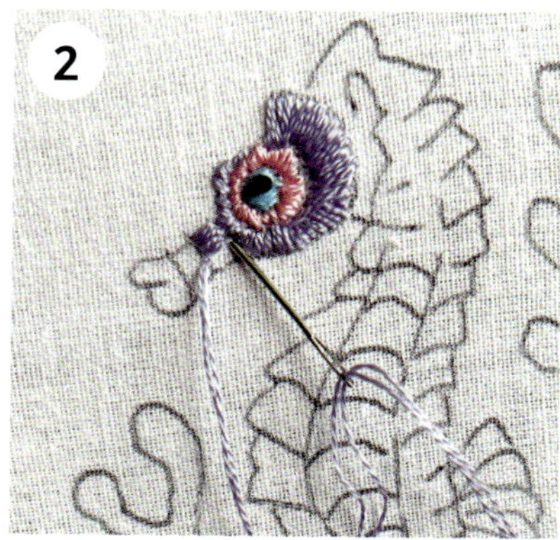

2

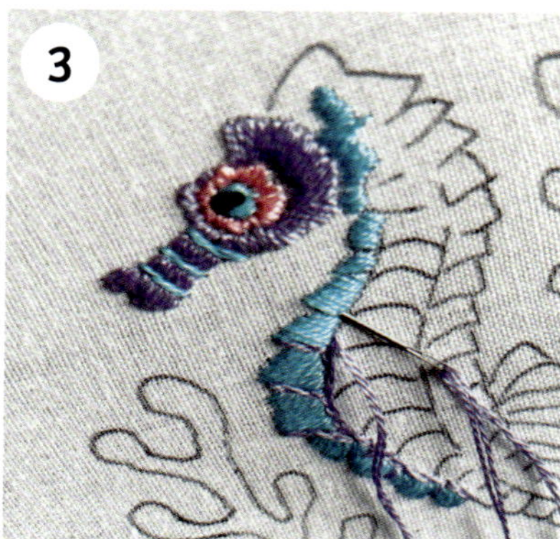

3

1. Use 3846 to fill in the eye with satin stitch and add a French knot in the centre with 310. Surround the eye with 894 in satin stitch.
2. Fill in the various segments of the face using 340 and satin stitch, then work split stitch along the divisions using 3846.
3. Begin to fill in the body segments, starting with those along the front, using 3846 in statin stitch, and work split stitch in between with 340. Repeat in the centre section, but changing the direction of the satin stitches to create an interesting texture.
4. Continue in statin stitch for the back section, using 741 to fill the segments and 608 for the dividing lines. Now use 742 for the fin on the back. For the tail, use 741 along inside half, filling in the outside half with 340.
5. Finally, still using satin stitch, fill in the pebbles using 894 and the seaweed using 3810.

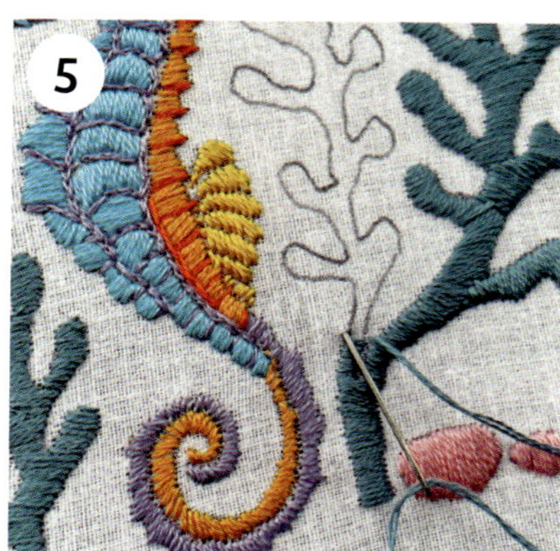

5

Motif 42:
Turtle

There are seven species of marine turtle. Each has a bony shell and long flippers, adapted for swimming. They make an interesting motif for embroidery – and you can choose natural colours or be more creative.

Thread colours

- 988 sage
- 840 sepia
- 907 lime
- 702 fern
- 645 dark grey

Use two strands of thread throughout.

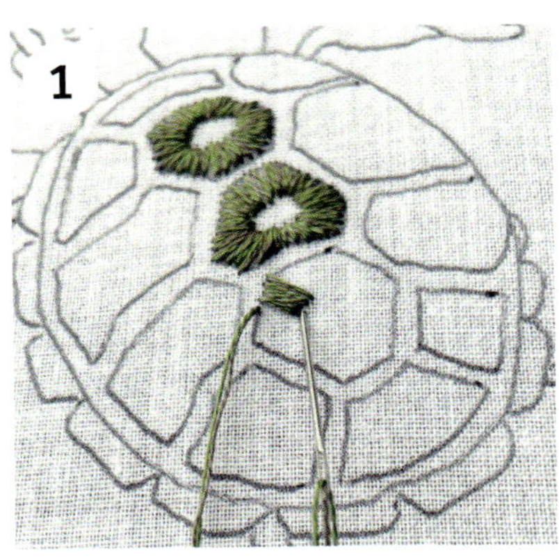

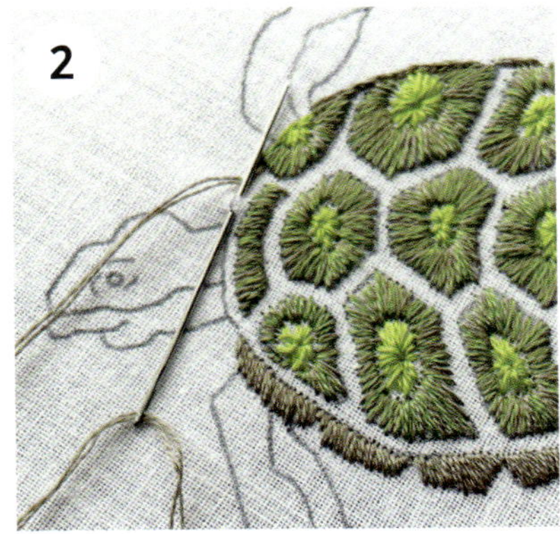

1. Start by filling in the shapes on the shell. Thread your needle with one strand of 988 and one strand of 840 and work satin stitch, taking the needle up through the outline of the shape and down towards the centre, leaving a central space unstitched.
2. Fill in the centres of the shapes with satin stitch using 907. Now fill in the shapes around the edge of the shell with 840 starting in satin stitch, but change to stem stitch to outline the top edge of the shell.
3. With one strand of 988 combined with one strand of 907, fill in the lower part of the head and the eye patch, as well as the lower part of each flipper, using satin stitch. Then, using 702, complete the head and flippers with split stitch filling.
4. Finally, using 645, emphasize the mouth with a few short stitches and create and eye with a French knot.

Creative ideas

You could enhance and expand this motif by adding seaweed, as in the Seahorse (page 66) or Fish (page 75), or some ripples of water, as in the Octopus (page 72).

Motif 43:
Crab

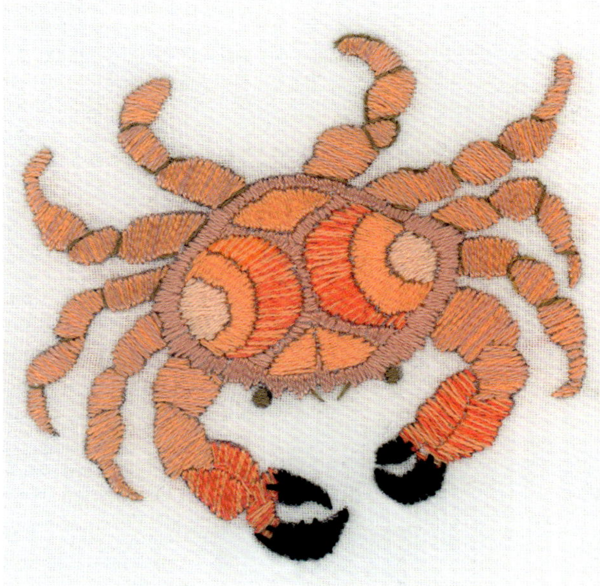

There are more than 4,500 species of crab. This stylized version is based on a brown crab, but you could embroider it in shades of blue, green, grey or other colours to depict other species.

Thread colours

- 891 watermelon
- 3341 peach
- 353 blush
- 760 salmon
- 310 black
- 840 sepia

Use two strands of thread throughout, unless otherwise stated.

1. Thread your needle with one strand of 891 and one strand of 3341. Fill in the two crescent shapes on the body of the crab with padded satin stitch, working close rows of small running stitches inside the shapes and covering these with satin stitch, working the stitches across the shapes.
2. Continuing in padded satin stitch, fill in the shapes at the top and bottom of the body, as well as those next to the inside curves of the crescents with 3341, then switch to 353 to fill in the far left and far right shapes of the body. Now fill in the remaining areas in 760 to complete the body.
3. For the legs, thread the needle with one strand of 3341 and one strand of 760 and work satin stitch across their width. Now use the same colour combination for the first two joints of each claw, then change to one strand of 3341 and one strand of 891 to continue the claws, and finally change again to two strands of 310 to complete their tips.
4. Using a single strand of 840, outline parts of the legs, particularly between the joints, in backstitch. Fill in the eyes with satin stitch and add two feelers.

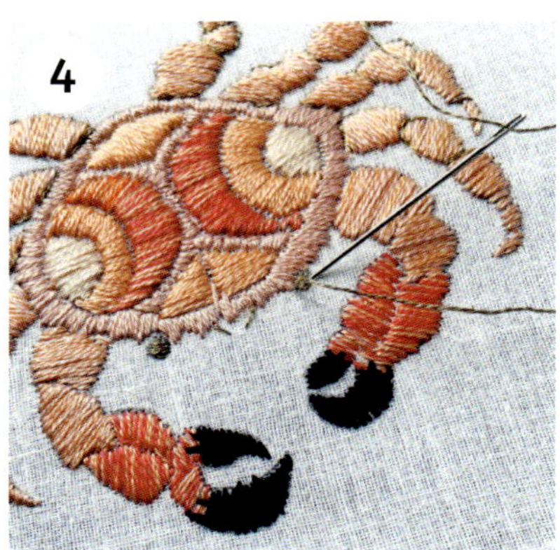

Notes on technique

This motif illustrates how effective satin stitch can be for filling small shapes. You could, if you prefer, fill the shapes with another stitch, such as split stitch filling, or you could simply outline the body, legs and claws, instead of filling them.

Motif 44: Lobster

Embroider this clawed crustacean in shades of red, as shown here, or in shades of brown, grey or blue.

Thread colours

- 891 watermelon
- 608 flame
- 347 russet
- 3341 peach
- 310 black

Use two strands of thread throughout.

1. Thread your needle with one strand of 891 and one strand of 608. Starting with the lobster's claws, fill in the shapes with padded satin stitch, laying a foundation of running stitches and covering these with satin stitch, worked across each shape.
2. With 347, stitch along the antennae and the lines on each side of the body, with split stitch, then fill in the body shell with split stitch filling, using a combination of one strand of 891 and one of 3341.
3. Fill in the tail and legs with 891 and satin stitch, followed by the tail with the 891 and 608 combination you used for the claws.
4. For the eyes, embroider two French knots in 310.

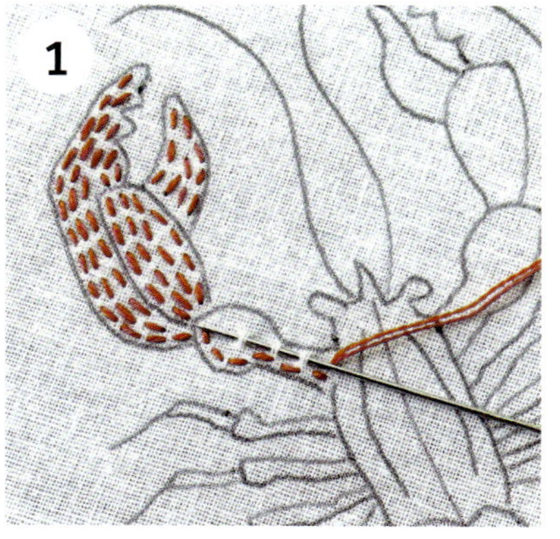

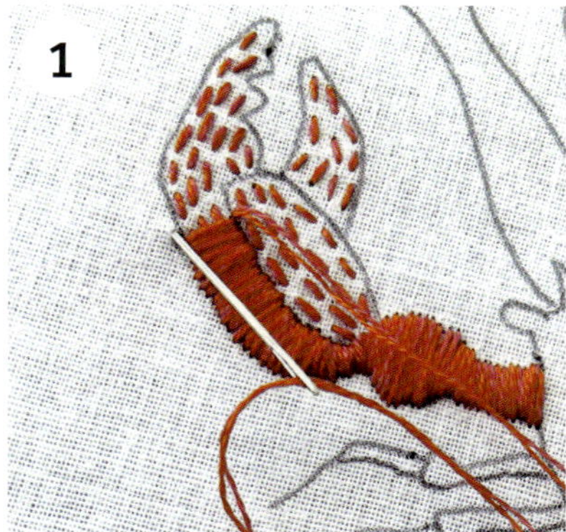

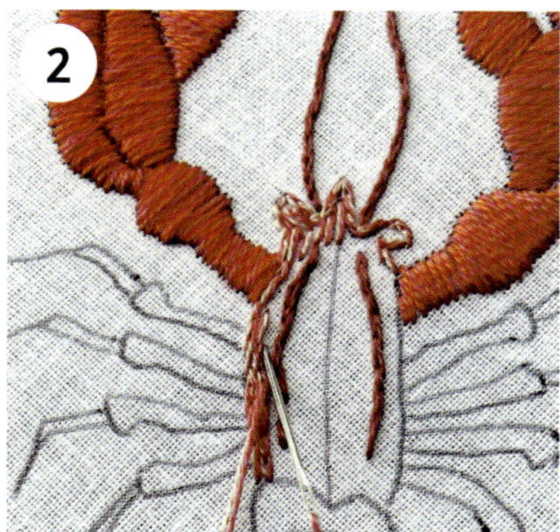

Notes on technique

Using padded satin stitch on the larger shapes helps with thread coverage, with the underlying foundation stitches helping to ensure that the white fabric doesn't show through the stitching.

Motif 45:
Prawns

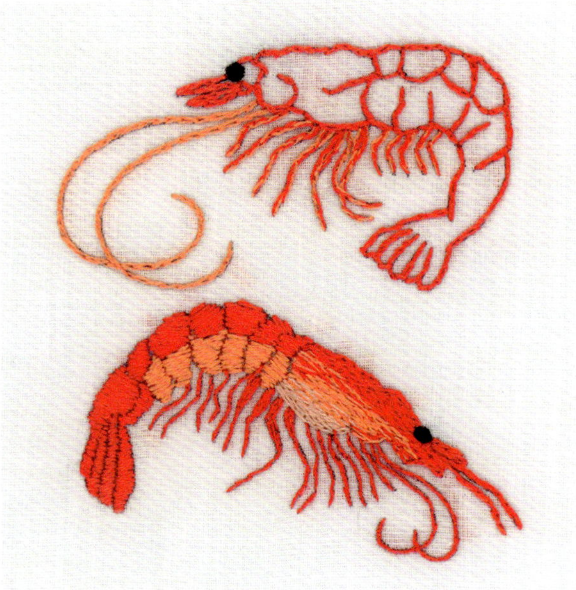

Prawns are native to every ocean on Earth; it's believed that the colder the water, the tastier the prawn. But these are for stitching, not for eating!

Thread colours

- 3341 peach
- 891 watermelon
- 310 black
- 353 blush

Use two strands of thread throughout, unless otherwise stated.

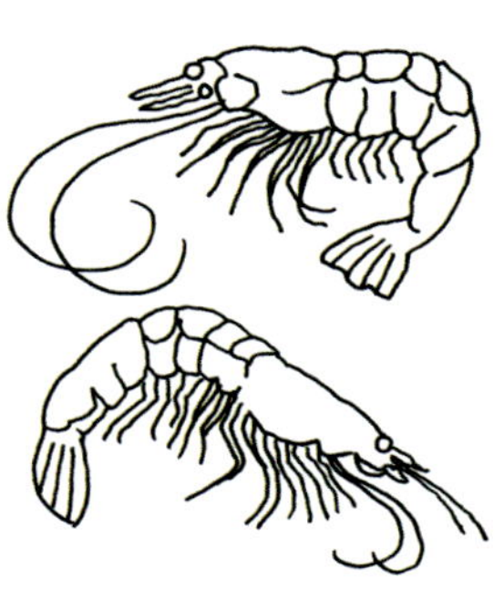

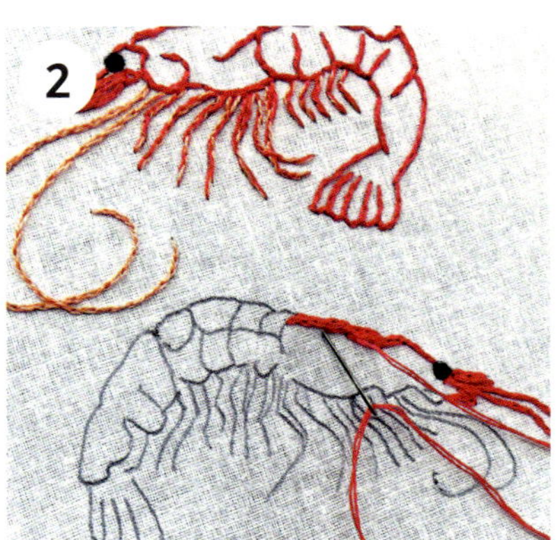

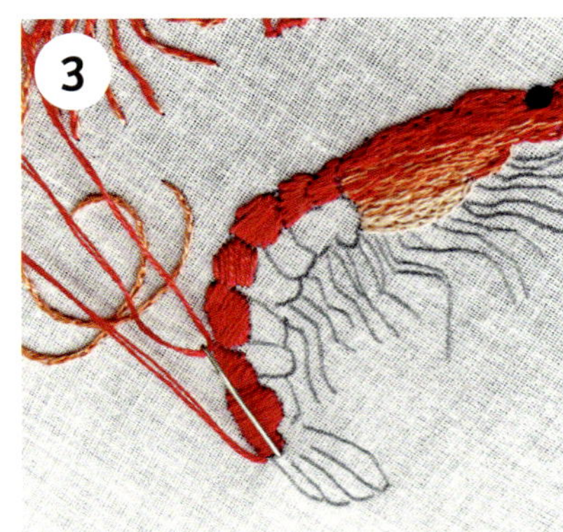

1. Stitch the outlines of the upper prawn in split stitch, using 3341 for the long antennae, 891 for the body and a combination of the two for the numerous legs. Fill in the eyes of both prawns with satin stitch and 310.
2. For the lower prawn, fill in the carapace with split stitch shading, starting at the top with two strands of 891, then one strand each of 891 and 3341, then 3341 alone, followed by 3341 and 353.
3. Fill in the segments that make up the abdomen using satin stitch, using 891 for the top segments and tail and 3341 for the lower segments.
4. Use 891 for the legs and antennae, using split stitch and a single strand.

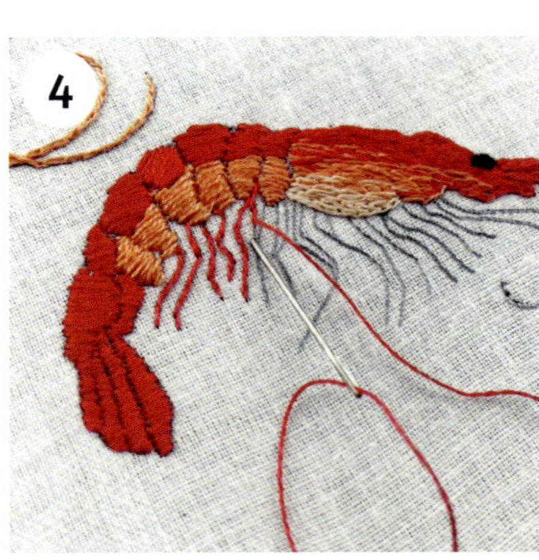

Creative ideas

Use one or two prawns to decorate the corner of a dinner napkin, place mat or tablecloth. Or combine them with other motifs, such as the Crab (page 68) and Lobster (page 69), to decorate a seafood bib or a beach bag.

Notes on technique

In the stitched example, each prawn has been embroidered in a different way – but you could, of course, stitch them in similar ways, choosing the method that appeals to you most.

Motif 46: Jellyfish

Jellyfish don't have brains, blood, eyes or even a heart. But they do have fascinating body shapes and tentacles that lend themselves extremely well to creative embroidery.

Thread colours

- 3810 sea green
- 3846 aqua
- 956 rose pink
- 3607 red-violet
- 340 lavender
- 894 candy pink
- 307 buttermilk

Use two strands of thread throughout.

1. Stitch along the interior lines on the body with 3810 and chain stitch, then fill in the areas in between with 3846 and split stitch filling.
2. Fill in the scalloped edge at the base of the body with 956 and satin stitch, then outline the lower edge with split stitch, using 3607.
3. Stitch along the narrowest tentacles with split stitch, using 3846. For the slightly wider tentacles use stem stitch – or a slanted version of satin stitch – with 340.
4. Fill in the frilly 'arms' with satin stitch, using 894, then outline each one in backstitch, using 956. Using 307, fill in the small circles at the ends of the tentacles with satin stitch. Finally, add a scattering of French knots in the same colour.

Creative ideas

Create an underwater scene by combining one or more Jellyfish with the Octopus (page 72) and perhaps the Fish (page 75) and Seahorse (page 66), adding extra seaweed fronds where needed.

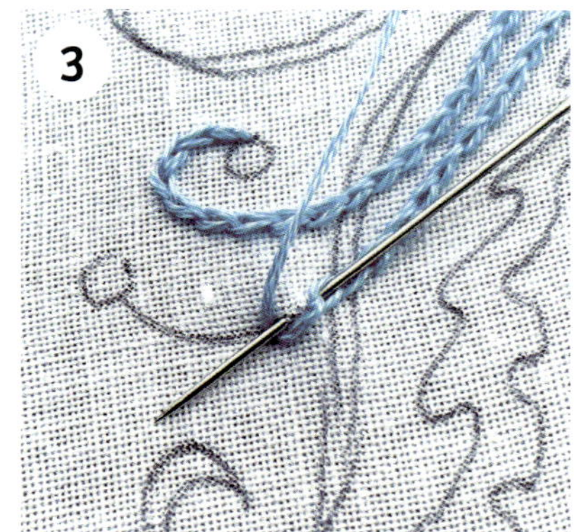

Motif 47: Octopus

With its rounded body and eight sinuous legs, this octopus motif could be embroidered using various combinations of stitches and a whole array of different colours – just use your creativity as well as your stitching skills.

Thread colours

- 891 watermelon
- 3846 aqua
- B5200 white
- 3341 peach
- 608 flame
- 3810 sea green

Use two strands of thread throughout.

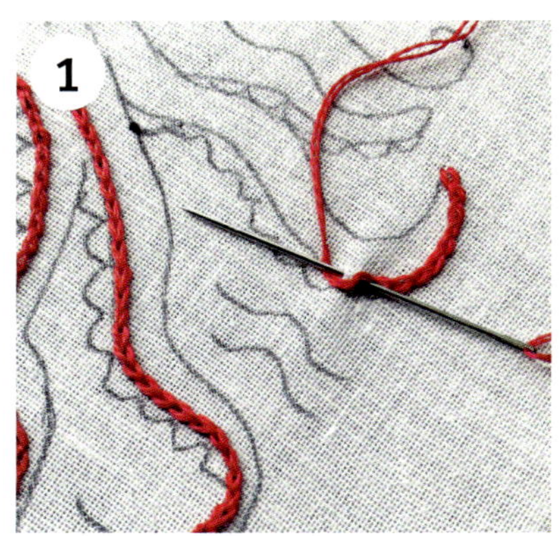

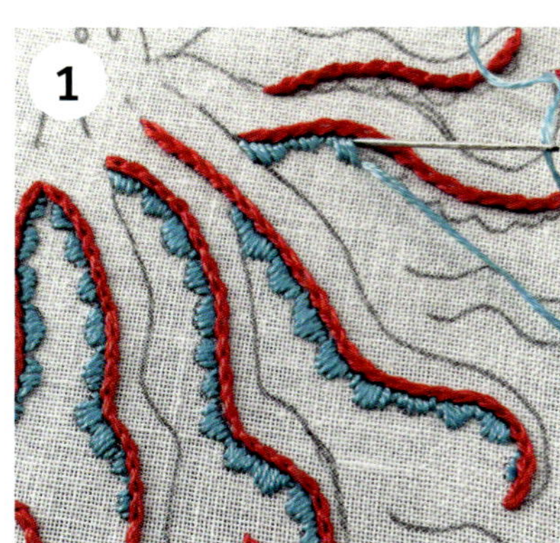

1. Using 891, outline the inner edge of each tentacle with chain stitch. Fill in the fluted edges – the suckers – with 3846 and satin stitch.
2. Using B5200, fill in the eyes with satin stitch then, using one strand of 3341 and one strand of 608 combined in the needle, fill in the rest of the tentacles and the body with split stitch filling.
3. Fill in the head in a similar way, this time using one strand of 891 and one strand of 608.
4. Finally, embroider the waves in 3810, using chain stitch, but to create a tapered end to each line, work the last two stitches in split stitch instead of chain stitch.

Notes on technique

Using two different colours at once – one strand of each – can create an interesting colour effect. Try it with your own colour combinations to see what different effects you can achieve.

Motif 48:
Dolphin

We are all familiar with the dolphin's playful nature. This one is depicted leaping high above the waves.

Thread colours

- ☐ B5200 white
- ■ 310 black
- ■ 927 grey
- ■ 799 cornflower
- ■ 645 dark grey
- ■ 3846 aqua

Use two strands of thread throughout.

1. Using satin stitch, fill in the small curved shape at the front of the head with B5200 and the eye with 310.
2. Fill in the central body shape, including the flipper, the centre of the dorsal fin and the centre of the tail flukes with split stitch filling, using 927. While you have that colour in your needle, stitch along the outline along the belly in split stitch.
3. Now fill in the belly and the beak with B5200. Fill in the top of the body in 799, still using split stitch filling. Next fill in the rest of the flukes and the front of the dorsal fin with 645. Add a few stitches with this colour to emphasize the beak.
4. Use 3846 to fill in the waves and water droplets in satin stitch, working the stitches at a slant.

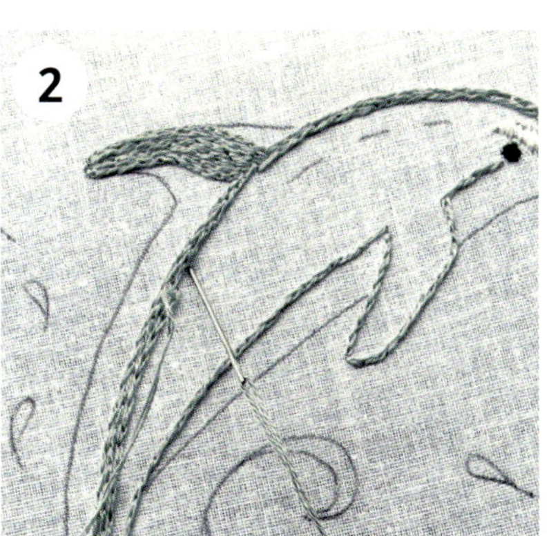

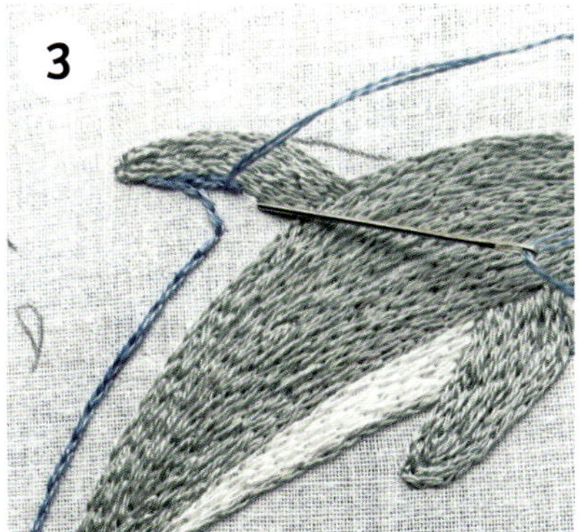

Motif 49: Starfish

This quirky sea creature has spiny skin covering its body and five arms – but it has no brain. That doesn't affect its decorative value, however.

Thread colours

- 3341 peach
- 742 apricot
- 746 ivory

Use two strands of thread throughout, unless otherwise stated.

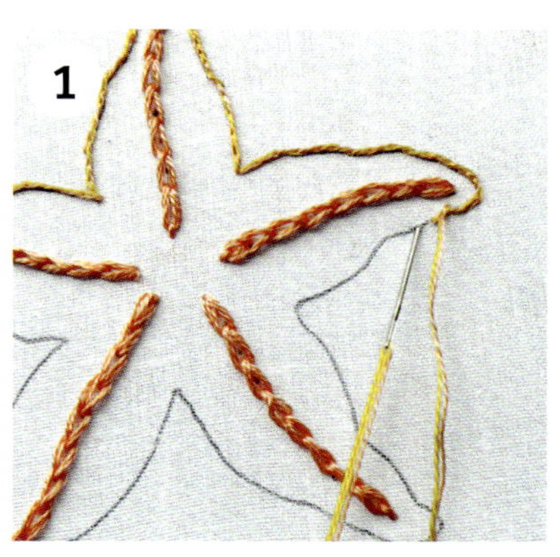

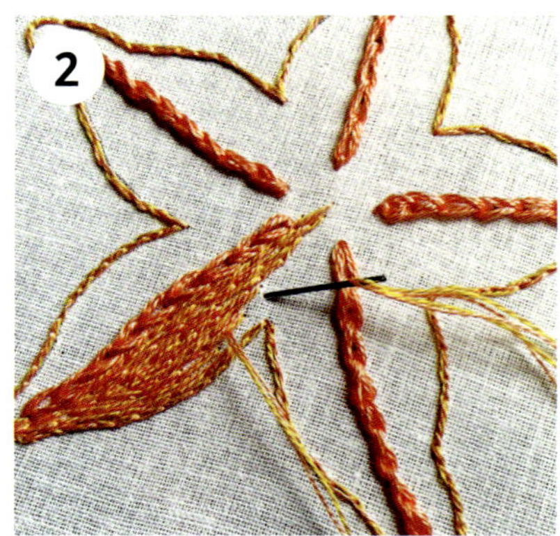

1. With four strands of 3341, embroider lines of chain stitch along the dotted lines inside the starfish. Next outline the whole shape with split stitch, using one strand of 3341 and one strand of 742 combined in your needle.
2. Now use the 3341 and 742 combination to fill in around the lines of chain stitch, stitching towards the outline using split stitch filling.
3. Using three strands of 746, work French knots along the chain stitched lines, bringing the needle up through the centre of each chain stitch.

Creative ideas

This would be a good motif to repeat, working each one in the same combination of colours or with different colours, depending on the effect you wish to achieve. It could also be combined with other Ocean motifs on items for the beach or the bathroom.

Motif 50: Fish

There are so many fish in the sea, of all shapes and sizes. This one represents them all, so you can use your imagination when stitching it.

Thread colours

- 563 pistachio
- 800 sky blue
- 210 lilac
- 894 candy pink
- 742 apricot
- 3846 aqua
- B5200 white

Use two strands of thread throughout.

1. Outline the fish in split stitch. Start with the head and two strands of 563, then change to one strand of 563 and one strand of 800 and continue around the body. When the thread runs out, swap to a combination of 800 and 210.
2. Once you have outlined the body and tail, go along the interior lines such as those for the fins, gill and mouth, using split stitch and changing colours as before and bringing 894 into the mix. Make the lateral line along the length of the body using running stitch.
3. For the fish's eye, fill in the outer ring with satin stitch and 742, then add a French knot in the centre using 3846.
4. Outline the bubbles with a combination of one strand of 3846 and one strand of B5200 in backstitch, using tiny stitches.
5. For the seaweed, using the 563 and 800 combination as well as the 800 and 210 combination, fill in the shapes with satin stitch.

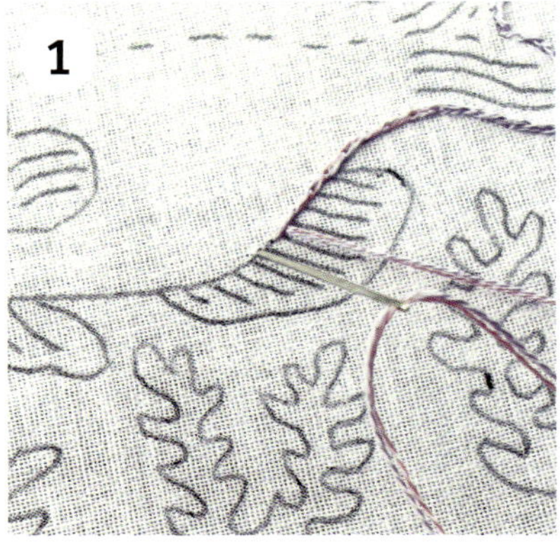

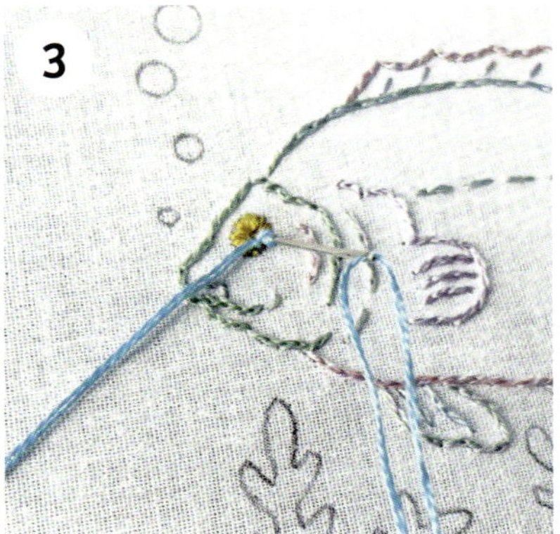

Motif 51:
Anchor

Nowadays anchors are available in an array of shapes and sizes to prevent boats drifting out to sea, but this anchor is in the traditional shape popularly used for hundreds of years.

Thread colours

- 927 grey
- 642 stone
- 436 cappuccino

Use two or three strands as stated.

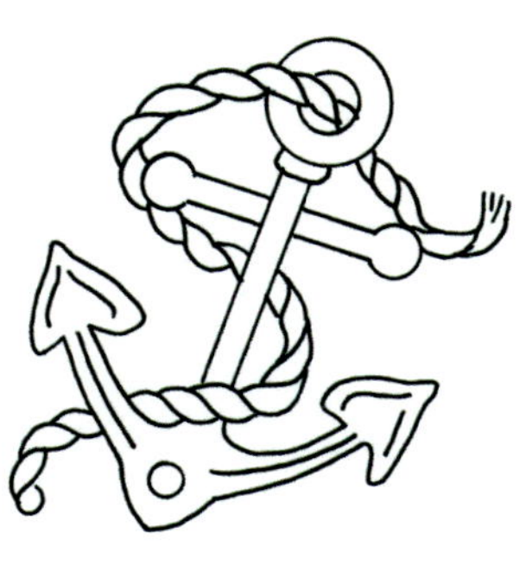

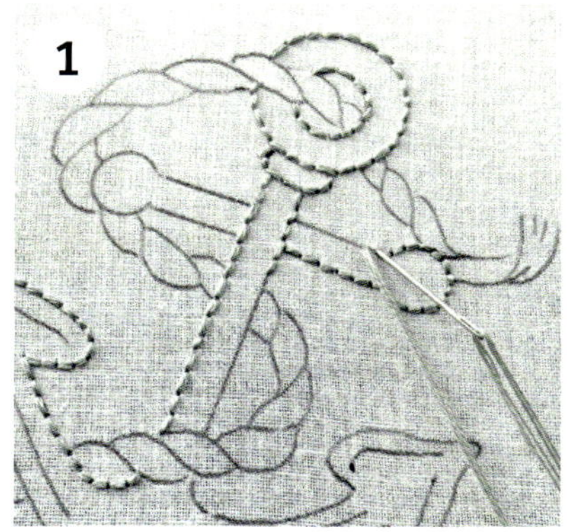

1. With three strands of 927, follow the outer lines of the anchor in backstitch, keeping the stitches small, then follow the inner lines using three strands of 642.
2. Using two strands of 436, fill in each small segment of the rope in satin stitch, with the stitches lying across the shapes.

Notes on technique

By outlining part of this motif, it's a quick motif to stitch – but if you have more time to spend, and plenty of thread, you could embroider the whole motif using filling stitches such as satin stitch or split stitch filling.

Motif 52: Sandcastle

Reminiscent of childhood days at the beach, this sandcastle can be embroidered in a number of different ways.

Thread colours

- 746 ivory
- 3046 beige
- 645 dark grey
- 869 cocoa
- 444 yellow
- 783 mustard
- 436 cappuccino
- 891 watermelon
- 3846 aqua

Use two strands of thread throughout.

1. Embroider the small internal details in the castle first. Using satin stitch, fill in the shell shape above the door with 746, the little pebbles on either side with 3046, the windows with 645 and the door with 869.
2. Fill in each section of the sandcastle with split stitch filling, working around the areas already embroidered first. Use one strand of 444 and one of 783 combined in the needle for the central section and the sections on either side.
3. For the turrets and towers, use split stitch filling in 444. Next, for the mound on which the castle stands, use 783 and long-and-short stitch, filling in one section at a time.
4. Using satin stitch, fill in the shaft of the spade with 436 and the handle and blade with 891. Use 891, too, to satin stitch the flags, then switch to 645 and backstitch for the sticks.
5. Finally, embroider the horizon line with 3846 and split stitch.

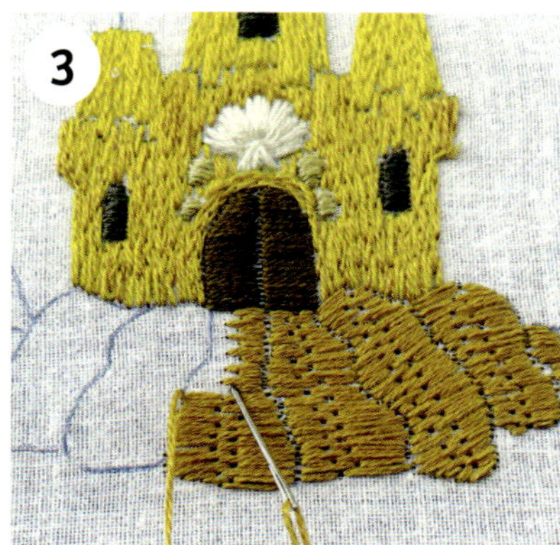

Motif 53:
Beach Umbrella

Choose sunny colours for this little beach scene of umbrella, towel and sunglasses, plus a few seagulls in flight.

Thread colours

- 436 cappuccino
- 740 orange
- 444 yellow
- 16 celery
- 645 dark grey
- 995 turquoise
- 927 grey

Use two strands of thread throughout.

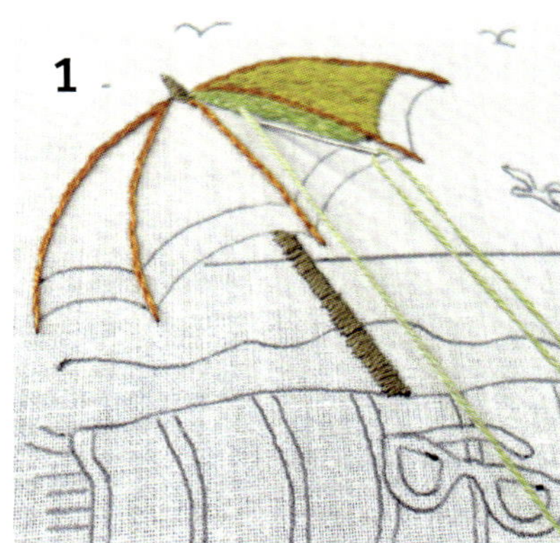

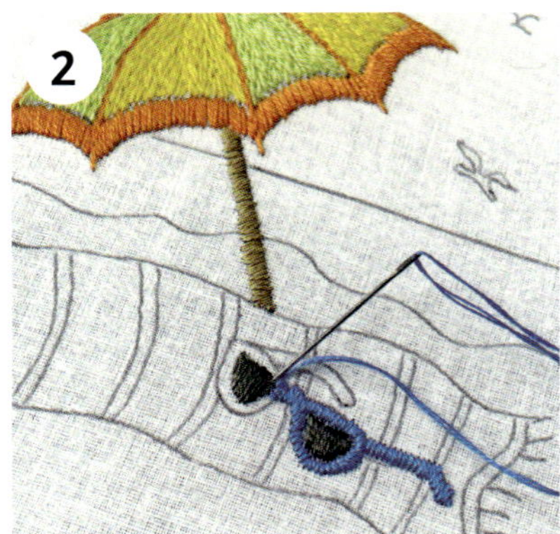

1. For the umbrella, use 436 to fill in the shaft with satin stitch. Now switch to 740 and outline the structure of the umbrella with split stitch, then fill in the areas in between with split stitch filling, using 444 and 16 for alternate segments. Finally, fill in the border trim with 740 and satin stitch.
2. Next, embroider the sunglasses in satin stitch, using 645 for the lenses and 995 for the frames.
3. For a co-ordinating towel, embroider the top and bottom edge in 444 and split stitch. Now use the same trio of colours that you used for the umbrella, working narrow satin stitch stripes in 740 and wider stripes in split stitch filling using 444 and 16. Stitch fringes using split stitch and 740.
4. Stitch the horizontal lines in split stitch: the horizon line with 995 and the wavy line with 444. Finally, continuing in split stitch, use 927 for the seagulls.

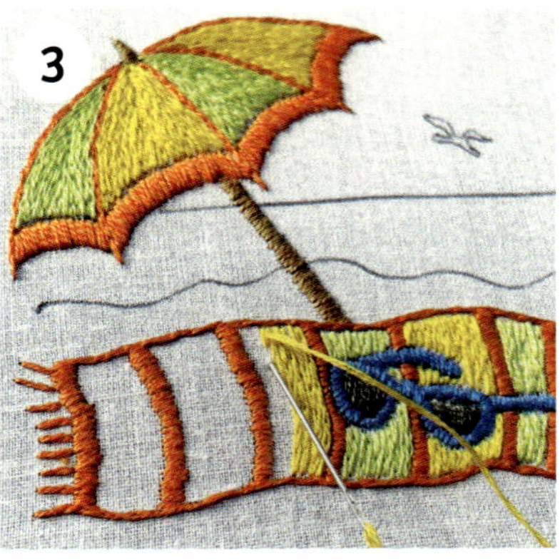

Creative ideas

This motif would look good on a beach bag, the corner of a beach towel or a custom-made sunglasses case.

Motif 54: Lighthouse

Encapsulated in a circular frame, here is a seaside scene featuring a lighthouse and setting sun.

Thread colours

- 3846 aqua
- 799 cornflower
- 783 mustard
- B5200 white
- 444 yellow
- 666 red
- 645 dark grey
- 988 sage

Use two strands of thread throughout.

1. Use split stitch and 3846 across the horizon. Next, use the same stitch to outline the circular border, using 799 for the upper half and 783 for the lower half.
2. Still using split stitch, describe the line of surf in B5200 and the sand in 783. For the sun use 444, filling in the semi-circle above the horizon with split stitch filling and using split stitch for the rays of sunshine.
3. Fill in the lighthouse in a similar way but with the stitch lines running vertically and horizontally and introducing 666 for the stripes and 645 for the windows.
4. Use 783 to trace the lines of the rocks in split stitch and to fill the pebbles with satin stitch. Complete the picture with straight stitches in 988 for the blades of grass.

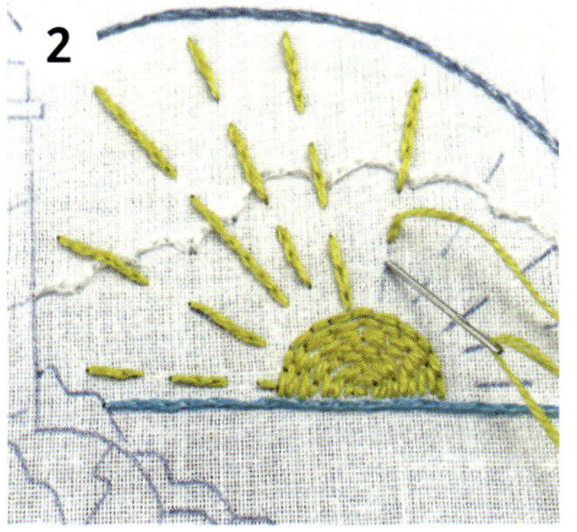

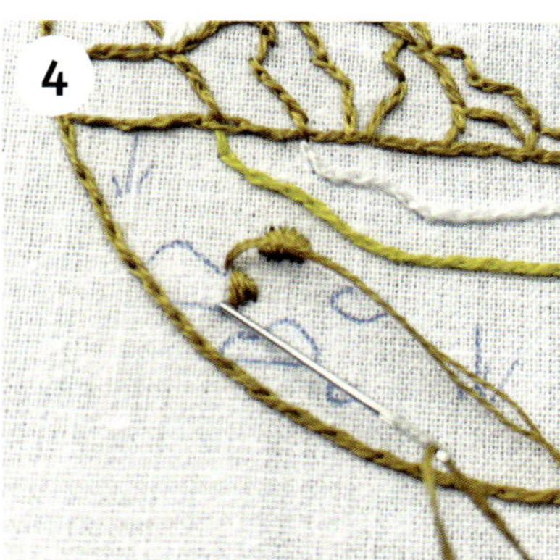

Creative ideas

Use this motif on the cover of a holiday album or to decorate a beach bag. It would also be perfect as the centrepiece of a patchwork quilt that features other sea-themed motifs.

Motif 55:
Weather Vane

Which way is the wind blowing? North, south, east or west? Weather vanes, which indicate the wind direction, are often decorated with a bird or animal, but this one has a sailing ship to lend it a nautical air.

Thread colours

- 645 dark grey
- 642 stone
- 927 grey
- 3042 heather

Use two strands of thread throughout.

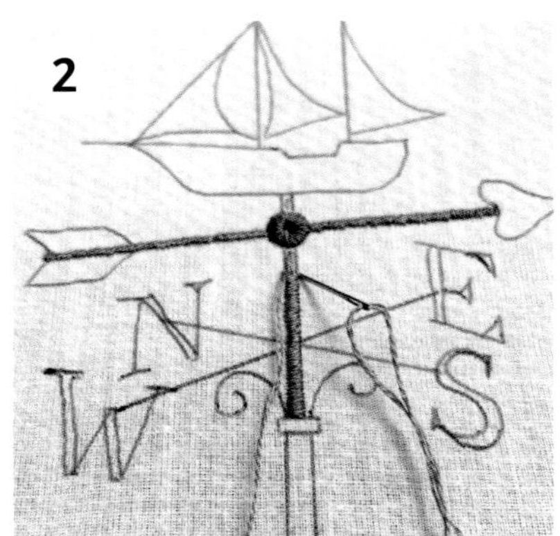
2

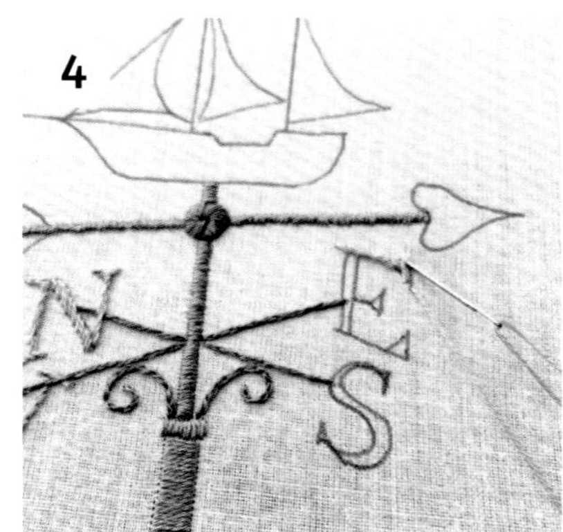
4

1. Fill in the circle in the centre of the arrow with 645 and satin stitch, working the stitches from the outline to the centre.
2. Using 642, fill in the upright post above the scrolls and the shaft of the arrow with overcast stitch. For the wider base of the post under the scrolls, you can use satin stitch.
3. Stitch along the horizontal bars – called directionals – with 645 and split stitch. Do the same with the scrolls.
4. Fill in the four letters with 927, using stem stitch for the narrower lines and satin stitch for the wider parts. Use the same thread colour and satin stitch for the ends of the arrow and for the sails of the ship.
5. Change to 3042 and satin stitch in the hull of the ship, then switch to 642 and split stitch in the masts and flags.

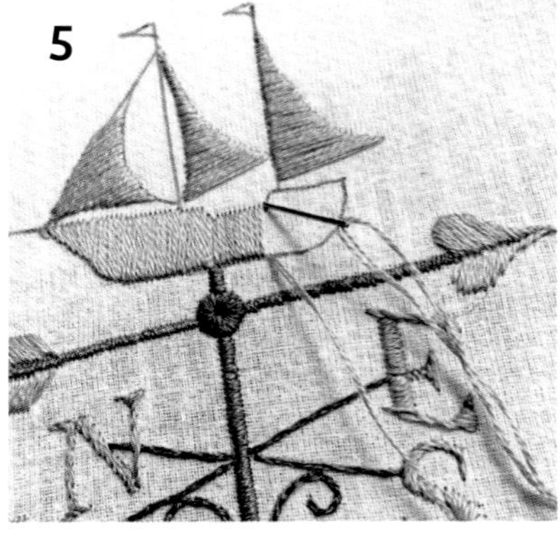
5

Creative ideas

Grey thread suggests a metal finish and, by choosing four subtle shades instead of just one colour you can introduce some visual interest.

Motif 56: Yacht

Is this little boat a dinghy, a sailing boat or a small yacht? While you are making up your mind, consider that this motif, when worked in outline stitches, is quick and easy to embroider.

Thread colours

- 3846 aqua
- 995 turquoise
- 642 stone
- 3042 heather
- 666 red

Use two strands of thread throughout.

1. Using 3846 and 995 separately for the waves, embroider the thinner curves of each one with stem stitch and the thicker areas with satin stitch, making a smooth transition from one to the other.
2. Switch to 642 and use overcast stitch for the mast. Next, use backstitch to outline the hull of the boat, the clouds and the seagulls. Now outline the sails in backstitch with 3042.
3. Fill in the flag at the top of the mast using satin stitch and 666. The sails can be left plain, or you can add a number or initials or other decoration, using a stitch and thread colour of your choice.

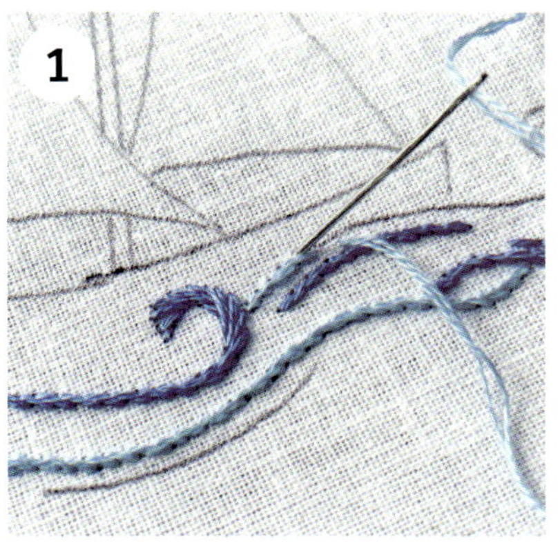

Notes on technique

Stem stitch can be considered to be a variation of satin stitch, with stitches worked along a narrow line and at a slant. Here, the two stitches combine very well to describe the varying thicknesses of the waves.

Motif 57:
Seashells

Seaweed fronds and a trio of shells of different shapes create a neat square that could form a central motif for a larger design.

Thread colours

- 605 shell pink
- 3046 beige
- 927 grey
- 436 cappuccino
- 783 mustard
- 3042 heather
- 563 pistachio

Use two strands of thread throughout, unless otherwise stated.

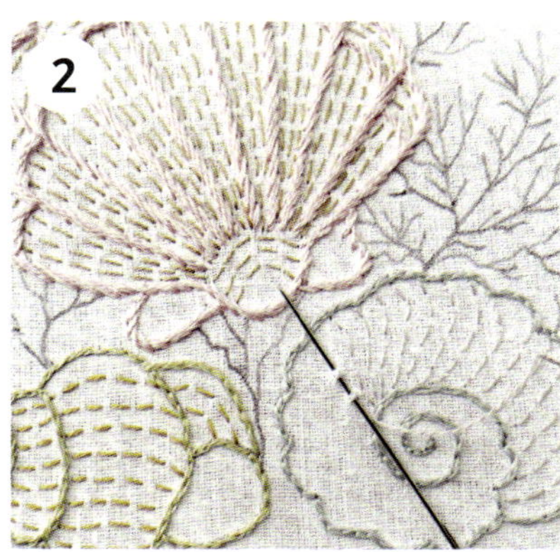

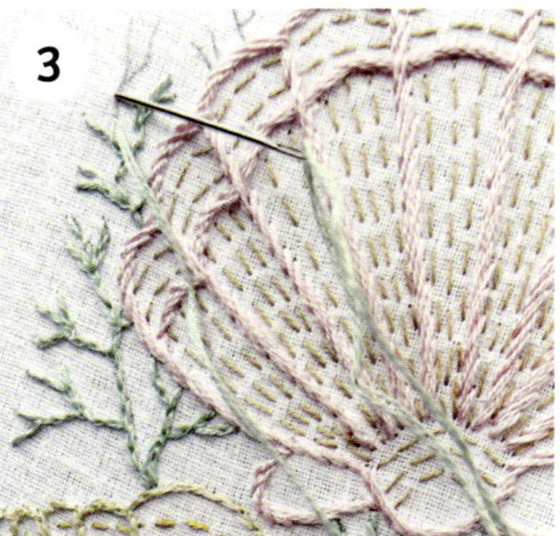

1. With 605 in the needle, follow all the outlines of the scallop shell with raised stem stitch, first working a foundation of backstitch and then going over this with stem stitch.
2. Outline the other two shells in split stitch, using 3046 and 927. Add further detail and texture to all the shells with lines of running stitch, worked freehand, using a single strand of 436 for the scallop shell, 783 for the snail and 3042 for the spiral shell.
3. For the fronds of seaweed, use two strands of 563 and split stitch.

Creative ideas

Many motifs allow you to add details of your own – and this is one of them. Here, extra lines have been added using a single strand of thread and running stitch, with the lines worked freehand. If you prefer to have guidelines to follow, use an erasable marker to add them, as running stitch will not cover the drawn lines.

Notes on technique

Stem stitch is one of the stitches that has a tendency to twist the thread as you work the stitches. To avoid tangles, remember to untwist it from time to time.

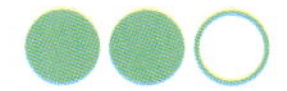

Motif 58: Palm Trees

These palm trees stand on a tiny tropical island, perfect for the would-be castaway.

Thread colours

- 3046 beige
- 307 buttermilk
- 783 mustard
- 702 fern
- 3846 aqua

Use two strands of thread throughout.

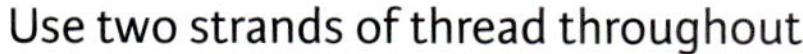

1. Thread your needle with one strand of 3046 and one strand of 307 and use this combination to fill in the sand with split stitch filling.
2. Embroider the trees with satin stitch, using 783 for the tree trunks and 702 for the palm leaves.
3. For the waves, start with satin stitch in 3846, but transition to stem stitch as they narrow.

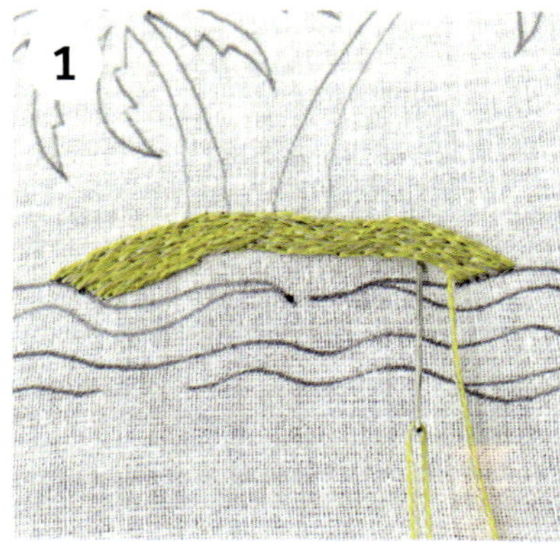

Creative ideas

Use this motif to decorate a holiday beach bag, passport sleeve or scrapbook cover.

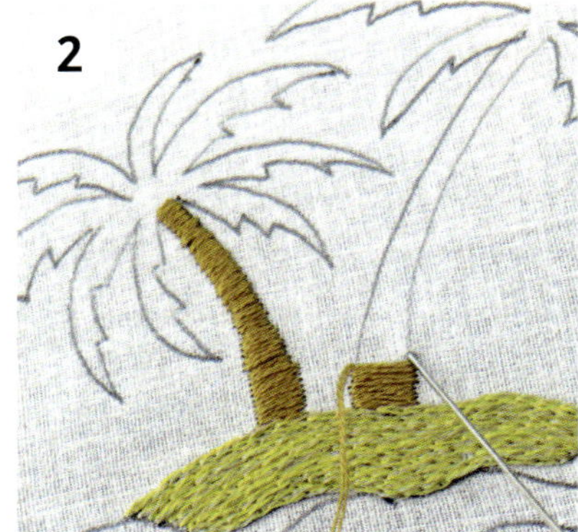

Motif 59:
Seagull

Commonly seen in seaside towns as well as in cities, where there are plentiful supplies of food to scavenge, seagulls are considered by many people to be a nuisance. They do tend to steal food, sometimes make loud squawking noises, and may even attack small pets.

Thread colours

- 645 dark grey
- B5200 white
- 927 grey
- 310 black
- 3341 peach
- 799 cornflower
- 444 yellow

Use two strands of thread throughout, unless otherwise stated.

1. Embroider the seagull's eye using 645 and a straight stitch with a French knot in the centre. Fill in the head and body using B5200 and split stitch filling.
2. Define the outline of the breast with split stitch and a single strand of 927. Now change to two strands of 927 and fill the far left area and central section of the wing with split stitch filling. Fill the remaining wing sections using 645 and 310.
3. Fill the legs with satin stitch in 3341. For the bollard, using 927, use split stitch filling in vertical rows, opening up the stitches towards the bottom to create broken colour.
4. For the horizon line, use split stitch and 799; for the cloud use the same stitch and 927. Finally, fill in the beak with satin stitch and 444.

Notes on technique

On the bollard, the solid colour is broken up at the base by opening up the stitches, working a few stitches with gaps in between like running stitch.

Motif 60:
Beach Huts

Oh, I do like to be beside the seaside! You can use your choice of colours to 'paint' these little wooden huts with thread.

Thread colours

- 436 cappuccino
- B5200 white
- 891 watermelon
- 642 stone
- 702 fern
- 800 sky blue
- 742 apricot
- 3810 sea green

Use two strands of thread throughout.

1. Working in satin stitch, fill in the steps and supports on both huts with 436. Then, starting with the right-hand hut, fill in the door using B5200 and the wooden planks alternately in B5200 and 891.
2. With 642, embroider the anchor in straight stitches and outline the door in backstitch. Continuing with the same colour, fill in the roof with satin stitch and stitch along the flag pole with split stitch. Fill in the flag with 702.
3. For the other hut, fill in the windows with 642 in satin stitch and the window sill and the rest of the door with B5200. Also use B5200 and straight stitches to make window bars. Complete this second hut in a similar way to the first, using B5200 and 800, and the flag in 891.
4. Stitch along the sand line with 742 and chain stitch. Finally, embroider the horizon line with 3810 and split stitch.

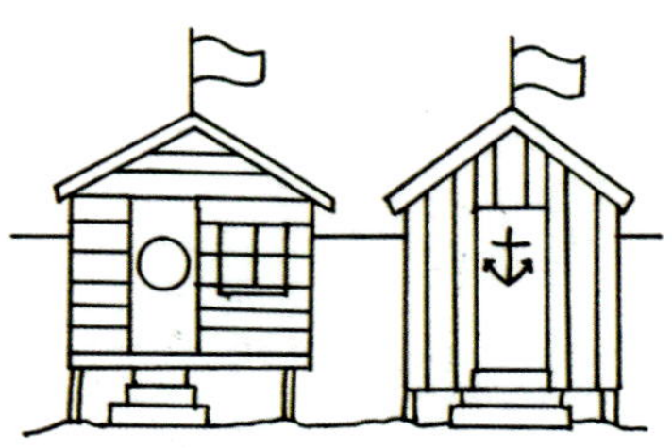

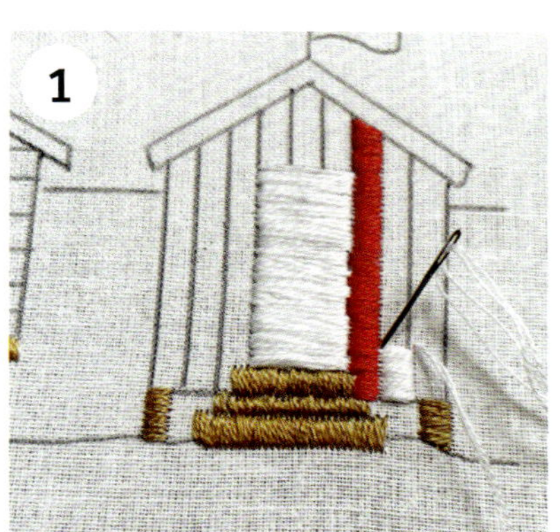

Motif 61:
Cottage

Quaint and cosy, with a flower-filled garden, this motif celebrates the quintessential English country cottage.

Thread colours

- 335 pomegranate
- 760 salmon
- 340 lavender
- 840 sepia
- 563 pistachio
- 742 apricot
- 3042 heather

Use two strands of thread throughout.

1. With 335 in the needle, outline the main parts of the house using three different stitches: split stitch for the base of the building, blanket stitch for the walls and satin stitch for the base of the roof.
2. Switch to 760 and fill in the rest of the roof in satin stitch. Using the same colour, embroider the path with small straight stitches to indicate paving stones.
3. Using 340, fill in the front door with satin stitch and outline the windows with overcast stitch. Finish the cottage but filling the chimney with satin stitch in 840.
4. Continuing with satin stitch and 840, fill in the tree trunk, then fill in the leafy parts of the tree with chain stitch and 563.
5. For the flowers, embroider each of the stalks in 563 with stem stitch. With 742, work five detached chain stitches radiating out from each marked dot to create petals. For each flower centre, work a French knot with 340. You can add a few extra blades of grass with 563, working small straight stitches around the tree and between the flowers.
6. For the smoke coming out of the chimney, use 3042 and split stitch. Continuing with the same thread colour, work a single straight stitch across each of the windows.

Motif 62: Shed

To be found in gardens and allotments everywhere, the garden shed provides storage for tools and, for some people, a sanctuary when some peace and quiet is needed.

Thread colours

- 645 dark grey
- 702 fern
- 701 emerald
- 436 cappuccino
- 3046 beige
- 746 ivory
- 3341 peach
- 891 watermelon

Use two strands of thread throughout.

1. With 645, fill in the door knob with satin stitch, working the stitches radiating out from the centre of the circle. Now fill in the boards that form the door using 702 and satin stitch, then fill in the door frame with 701, also using satin stitch.
2. Fill in the planks that make up the shed using a combination of one strand of 436 with one of 3046 and working the satin stitches in different directions. At the same time, fill in the piece of paper pinned to the shed, using 746, adding French knot 'pins' in 645.
3. For the flowerpot, use one strand of 436 with one strand of 3341: for the body of the pot use long-and-short stitch and for the rim use satin stitch. Then embroider the flower stems and leaves in stem stitch with 702 and the flower heads in 891 and satin stitch.
4. For the roof, use 645 and satin stitch and, finally, for the spade use satin stitch again, with 436 for the shaft and 891 for the handle and blade.

Notes on technique

Use the weave of the fabric as a guide to keep the edges nice and straight.

Motif 63:
Garden Gate

This can be used to depict a welcome to your home or to celebrate moving to a new home.

Thread colours

- 642 stone
- 703 shamrock
- 943 pine green
- 891 watermelon
- 783 mustard
- 869 cocoa
- 800 sky blue

Use two strands of thread throughout, unless otherwise stated.

1. Fill in the pebbles with satin stitch and 642 and the tufts of grass with 703, then complete the whole gate with 943, starting with the gateposts and horizontal bars.
2. For the plants on the left, use 703 to stitch the stems in stem stitch and the leaves in satin stitch. For the round flower heads, use 891.
3. For the plant pot, use 783 and satin stitch for the rim and split stitch for the rest of the pot. For the trunk of the tree, use 869 and satin stitch.
4. For the fruit and foliage, first use 891 and satin stitch for the fruit and then fill in the leaves with split stitch filling and 703.
5. Fill in the butterfly wings using satin stitch and 800, adding details with one strand of 642 and a few small stitches.

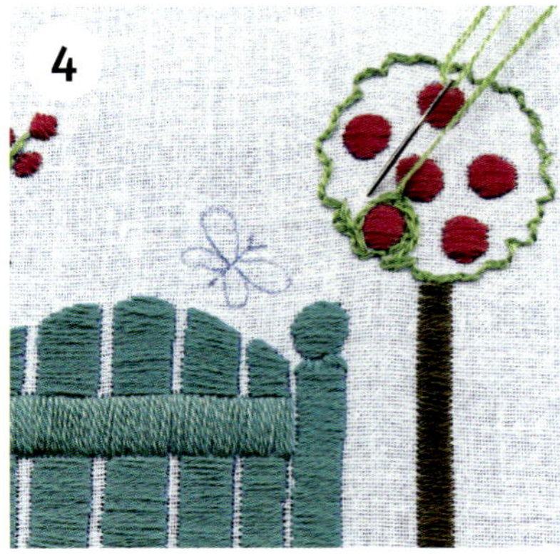

Creative ideas

Use this motif to embellish a gift – such as a framed picture, a little bag or cushion – for a gardener or for someone who has just moved into a new home.

Motif 64:
Washing Line

Baby clothes, freshly washed and hung out to dry, are fluttering in the breeze. This motif is just the thing for a baby gift or birth announcement card.

Thread colours

- 840 sepia
- 799 cornflower
- 353 blush
- 3806 fuchsia
- 605 shell pink
- 746 ivory
- 702 fern
- 927 grey

Use two strands of thread throughout, unless otherwise stated.

1. With three strands of 840, sew backstitch along the washing line.
2. For the playsuit, you can fill it in with one colour or customize it. For stripes, you can either draw guidelines or work freehand. Using satin stitch, fill in the yoke and the sleeves with 799 and alternate with 353 for making stripes.
3. For the dress, use 3806 and satin stitch to fill in the heart shape, then use 605 to fill in the rest of the bodice and each of the sections of the skirt. Finish the dress with a narrow satin stitch hem using 3806.
4. For the socks, use satin stitch with 746 for the main part and 3806 for the toes, heels and tops.
5. Using stem stitch and 702, stitch along the horizon line and the blades of grass. Finally, use 927 and a few small straight stitches to denote the pegs.

Creative ideas

In this embroidered sample, the central garment has been customized with stripes. You could just as easily add a number or initial to personalize your version.

Motif 65:
Tree

A simple motif like this strong, sturdy tree on a hillside has all sorts of applications, for all kinds of occasions.

Thread colours

- 840 sepia
- 436 cappuccino
- 703 shamrock
- 907 lime

Use two strands of thread throughout.

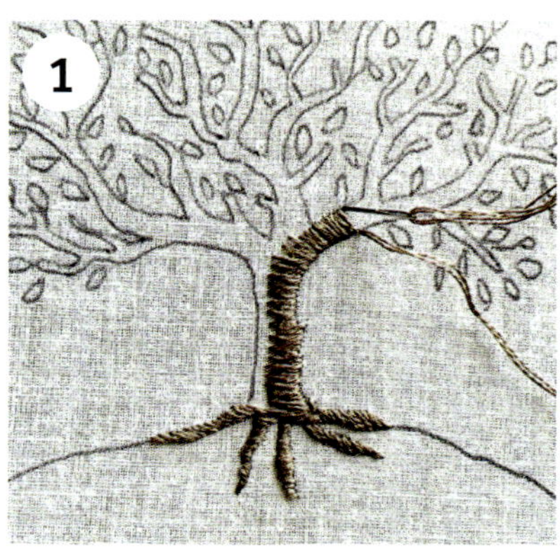

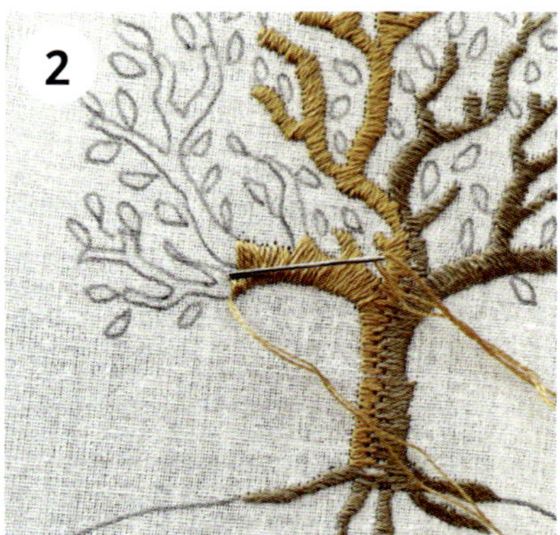

1. Using 840, fill in the tree roots with satin stitch. Now, working on the right-hand side of the motif and moving upwards, use long-and-short stitch on the trunk, changing back to satin stitch as you reach the branches and stem stitch for the thinner twigs.
2. Change the thread to 436 and complete the left-hand side of the trunk and the branches.
3. Fill in the leaves with satin stitch: use 703 for those on the right-hand side and 907 for those on the left. You will need just three or four small stitches for each leaf.
4. Finally, outline the hill with stem stitch and 702.

Notes on technique

You may prefer to embroider each leaf with a detached chain stitch, in which case it is advisable to draw the design on the fabric using an erasable marker, so that the marks can be removed after stitching.

Creative ideas

You could embroider four of these motifs to represent the seasons, using russet shades for the autumn (fall) leaves and omitting the leaves altogether for winter. For spring, you could add a scattering of French knots in shades of pink and white.

Motif 62: Shed

To be found in gardens and allotments everywhere, the garden shed provides storage for tools and, for some people, a sanctuary when some peace and quiet is needed.

Thread colours

- 645 dark grey
- 702 fern
- 701 emerald
- 436 cappuccino
- 3046 beige
- 746 ivory
- 3341 peach
- 891 watermelon

Use two strands of thread throughout.

1. With 645, fill in the door knob with satin stitch, working the stitches radiating out from the centre of the circle. Now fill in the boards that form the door using 702 and satin stitch, then fill in the door frame with 701, also using satin stitch.
2. Fill in the planks that make up the shed using a combination of one strand of 436 with one of 3046 and working the satin stitches in different directions. At the same time, fill in the piece of paper pinned to the shed, using 746, adding French knot 'pins' in 645.
3. For the flowerpot, use one strand of 436 with one strand of 3341: for the body of the pot use long-and-short stitch and for the rim use satin stitch. Then embroider the flower stems and leaves in stem stitch with 702 and the flower heads in 891 and satin stitch.
4. For the roof, use 645 and satin stitch and, finally, for the spade use satin stitch again, with 436 for the shaft and 891 for the handle and blade.

Notes on technique

Use the weave of the fabric as a guide to keep the edges nice and straight.

Motif 63:
Garden Gate

This can be used to depict a welcome to your home or to celebrate moving to a new home.

Thread colours

- 642 stone
- 703 shamrock
- 943 pine green
- 891 watermelon
- 783 mustard
- 869 cocoa
- 800 sky blue

Use two strands of thread throughout, unless otherwise stated.

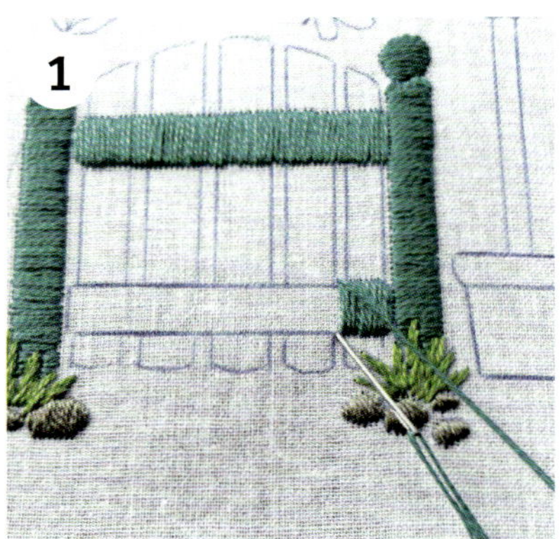

1. Fill in the pebbles with satin stitch and 642 and the tufts of grass with 703, then complete the whole gate with 943, starting with the gateposts and horizontal bars.
2. For the plants on the left, use 703 to stitch the stems in stem stitch and the leaves in satin stitch. For the round flower heads, use 891.
3. For the plant pot, use 783 and satin stitch for the rim and split stitch for the rest of the pot. For the trunk of the tree, use 869 and satin stitch.
4. For the fruit and foliage, first use 891 and satin stitch for the fruit and then fill in the leaves with split stitch filling and 703.
5. Fill in the butterfly wings using satin stitch and 800, adding details with one strand of 642 and a few small stitches.

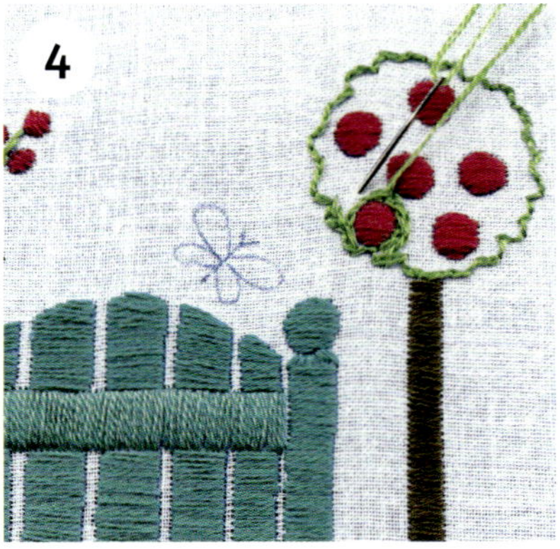

Creative ideas

Use this motif to embellish a gift – such as a framed picture, a little bag or cushion – for a gardener or for someone who has just moved into a new home.

Motif 64: Washing Line

Baby clothes, freshly washed and hung out to dry, are fluttering in the breeze. This motif is just the thing for a baby gift or birth announcement card.

Thread colours

- 840 sepia
- 799 cornflower
- 353 blush
- 3806 fuchsia
- 605 shell pink
- 746 ivory
- 702 fern
- 927 grey

Use two strands of thread throughout, unless otherwise stated.

1. With three strands of 840, sew backstitch along the washing line.
2. For the playsuit, you can fill it in with one colour or customize it. For stripes, you can either draw guidelines or work freehand. Using satin stitch, fill in the yoke and the sleeves with 799 and alternate with 353 for making stripes.
3. For the dress, use 3806 and satin stitch to fill in the heart shape, then use 605 to fill in the rest of the bodice and each of the sections of the skirt. Finish the dress with a narrow satin stitch hem using 3806.
4. For the socks, use satin stitch with 746 for the main part and 3806 for the toes, heels and tops.
5. Using stem stitch and 702, stitch along the horizon line and the blades of grass. Finally, use 927 and a few small straight stitches to denote the pegs.

Creative ideas

In this embroidered sample, the central garment has been customized with stripes. You could just as easily add a number or initial to personalize your version.

Motif 65:
Tree

A simple motif like this strong, sturdy tree on a hillside has all sorts of applications, for all kinds of occasions.

Thread colours

- 840 sepia
- 436 cappuccino
- 703 shamrock
- 907 lime

Use two strands of thread throughout.

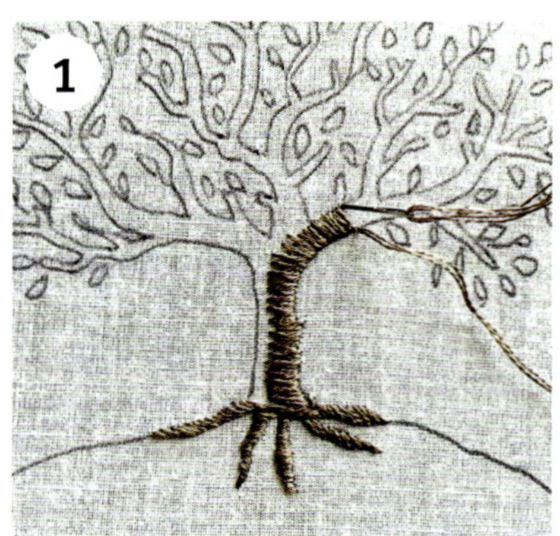

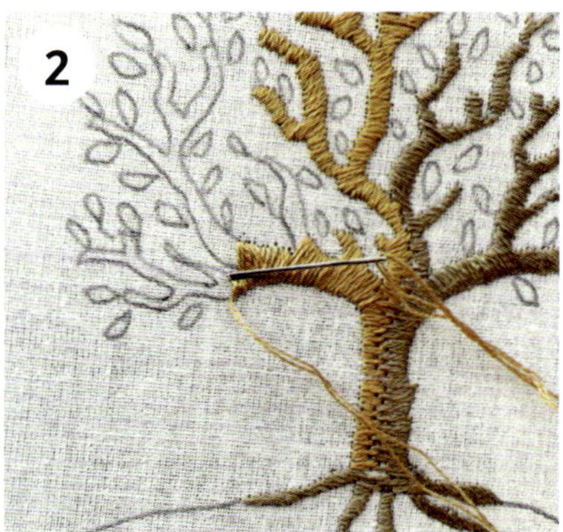

1. Using 840, fill in the tree roots with satin stitch. Now, working on the right-hand side of the motif and moving upwards, use long-and-short stitch on the trunk, changing back to satin stitch as you reach the branches and stem stitch for the thinner twigs.
2. Change the thread to 436 and complete the left-hand side of the trunk and the branches.
3. Fill in the leaves with satin stitch: use 703 for those on the right-hand side and 907 for those on the left. You will need just three or four small stitches for each leaf.
4. Finally, outline the hill with stem stitch and 702.

Notes on technique

You may prefer to embroider each leaf with a detached chain stitch, in which case it is advisable to draw the design on the fabric using an erasable marker, so that the marks can be removed after stitching.

Creative ideas

You could embroider four of these motifs to represent the seasons, using russet shades for the autumn (fall) leaves and omitting the leaves altogether for winter. For spring, you could add a scattering of French knots in shades of pink and white.

Motif 66:
Flower Basket

This pretty gift basket features a variety of pretty flowers and leaves, perfect for customization with your favourite colours.

Thread colours

- 3806 fuchsia
- 783 mustard
- 3046 beige
- 210 lilac
- 444 yellow
- 3341 peach
- 702 fern
- 907 lime

Use two strands of thread throughout.

1. Using 3806 and satin stitch, fill in the petals of the rose, working from the centre outwards.
2. Thread your needle with one strand each of 783 and 3046 and fill in the base and rim of the basket using satin stitch and the criss-crossing lines with chain stitch. Also use satin stitch to fill in the handle. For the bow on the handle, use 210 and satin stitch.
3. Continuing with satin stitch, fill in the flower centres with 444, then the petals of the two larger flowers with 3341 and the smaller flowers with 210.
4. Embroider the stems of the flowers with stem stitch and 702, and the leaves with the same colour thread and satin stitch. Also fill in the small gaps within the basket.
5. Finally, embroider the leafy stems with 907, using stem stitch for the stems and satin stitch for the leaves.

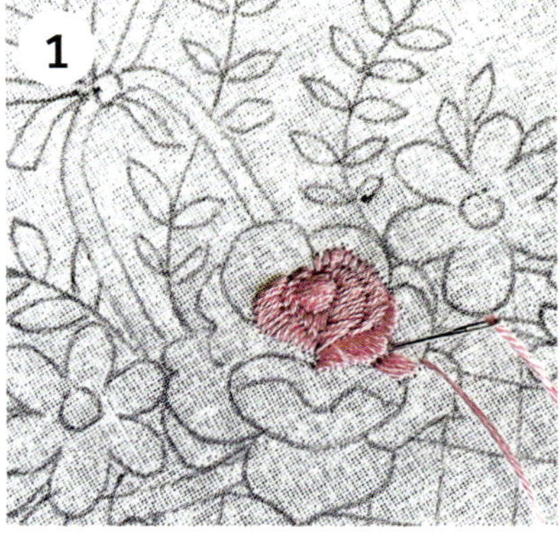

Creative ideas

This would make a pretty central motif for a cushion. You could surround it with repeats of the Rose motif (page 54).

Motif 67:
Beehive

A beehive is a man-made structure to house bees. Modern hives are made from wood or plastic but here's an old-fashioned one, called a skep, that is made from wicker.

Thread colours

- 783 mustard
- 840 sepia
- 3046 beige
- 702 fern
- 3806 fuchsia
- 340 lavender
- 444 yellow
- 645 dark grey
- 927 grey

Use two strands of thread throughout, unless otherwise stated.

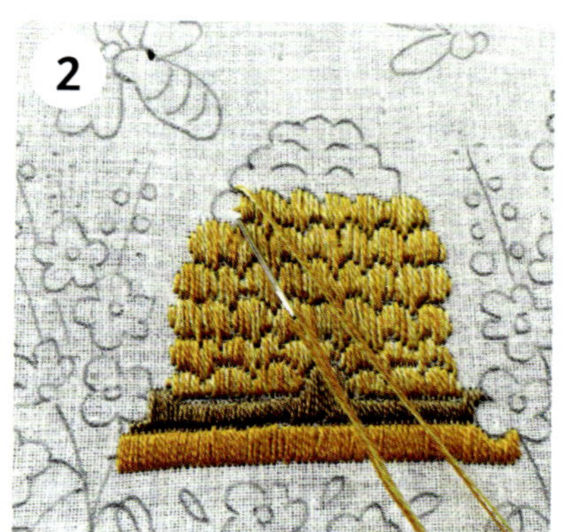

1. Using satin stitch, fill in the base strip of the beehive with 783 and the section above, including the entrance, in 840.
2. Now work each layer of the beehive, from the bottom upwards, with one strand of 3046 combined with one strand of 783.
3. Using 702, stitch along all the stems in split stitch and fill in the leaves with satin stitch. Now fill in all the flower petals using 3806 and satin stitch and the small circles and dots using 340 and satin stitch or French knots.
4. For the bees, use satin stitch for the bodies, working stripes of 444 and 645. Outline the wings with 927 and backstitch, then add legs and antennae with a single strand of 645.

Creative ideas

You could partner this motif with the Birds and Bees (page 43) or Cottage (page 86). Or use it to decorate a fabric cover for a jar of honey.

Motif 68: Sewing Machine

This old-fashioned sewing machine will appeal to anyone who enjoys needlework – and it is an appropriate subject for stitching.

Thread colours

- 800 sky blue
- 799 cornflower
- 927 grey
- 645 dark grey
- 436 cappuccino
- 608 flame

Use two strands of thread throughout, unless otherwise stated.

1. Using 800, fill in the small central circle with satin stitch, taking stitches from the edge of the circle to the centre.
2. Fill in the outer ring with 799 and padded satin stitch, starting with a foundation of several rows of running stitch.
3. Using the two shades of blue – 800 and 799 – fill in some of the other shapes using satin stitch, introducing 927 for the needle, the spool pin and parts of the hand wheel.
4. Use three strands of 645 to outline the machine in backstitch and to complete tiny details.
5. Fill in the top and base of the spool of thread with 436 and satin stitch. Embroider the thread with 608, firstly using satin stitch to make horizontal lines on the spool, keeping the lines close together, then changing to stem stitch for the line of thread leading from the spool to the needle.

Notes on technique

To keep the edges straight when working satin stitch on the narrow horizontal and vertical strips, try to follow the grain of the fabric: the warp and weft threads. This means that when you are drawing out the initial design, you should try to ensure that the straight lines are drawn along the threads of the fabric.

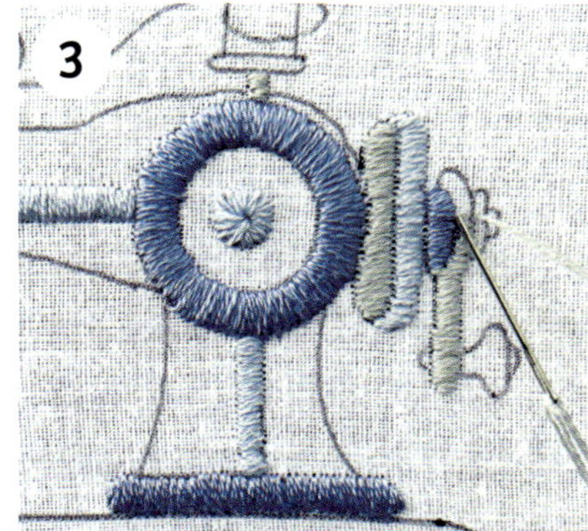

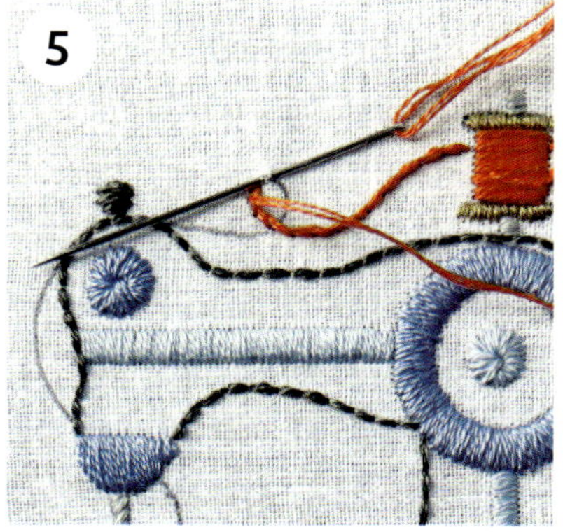

Motif 69:
Needlework

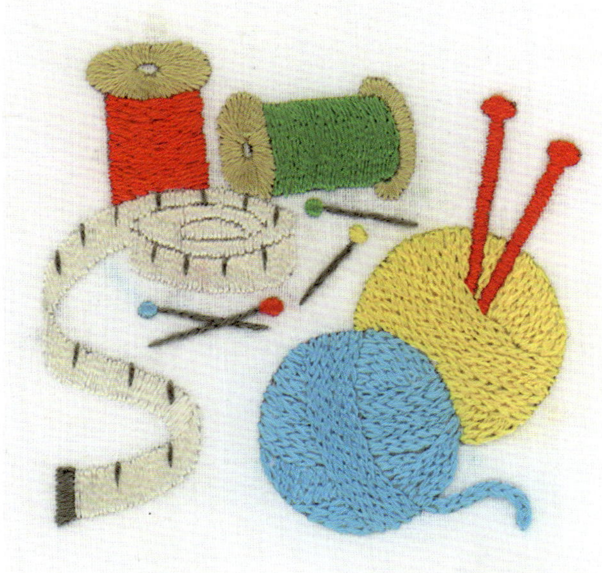

Needlework is a popular hobby, and lots of homes have a workbasket or drawer stocked with needles and threads and other items like those shown here.

Thread colours

- 746 ivory
- 645 dark grey
- 666 red
- 444 yellow
- 702 fern
- 3846 aqua
- 3046 beige

Use two strands of thread throughout.

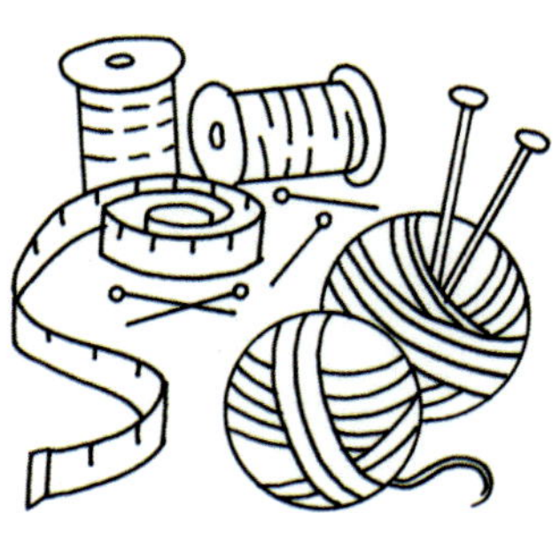

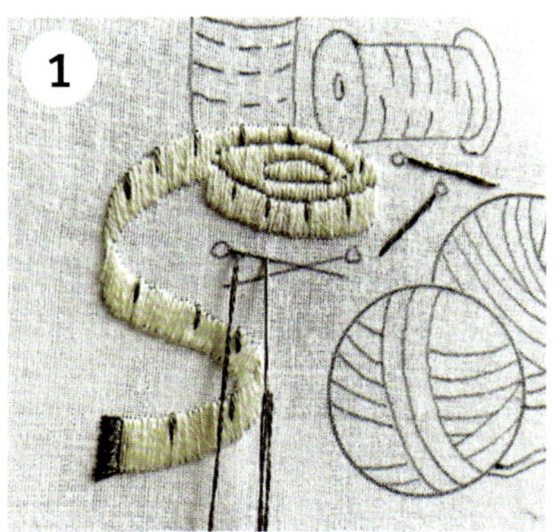

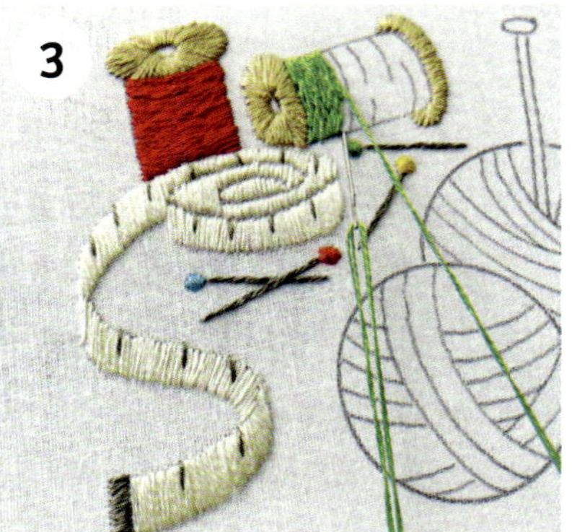

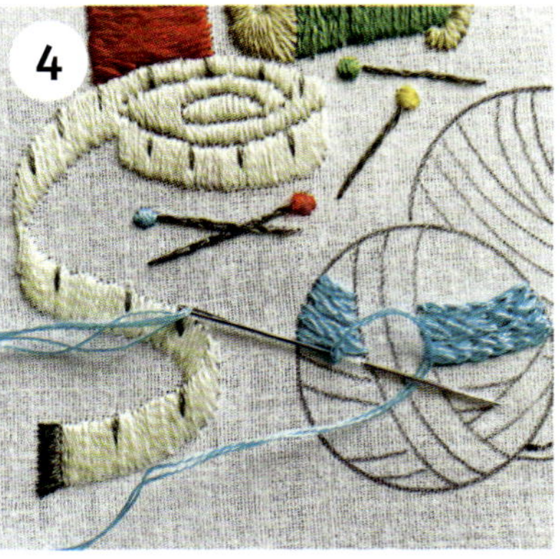

1. Fill in the tape measure using 746 and satin stitch, with the stitches going across the width of the tape. Change to 645 and fill in the end of the tape measure in satin stitch, then work the markings on the tape with single straight stitches and the shafts of the pins in split stitch.
2. Fill in the pin heads with satin stitch in various colours: 666, 444, 702 and 3846. Next, fill in the ends of the spools of thread using 3046 and satin stitch.
3. Embroider the thread on the reels with neat rows of split stitch, following the contours of the reels, indicated by the curved lines. Use 666 for one of the reels and 702 for the other, or use your own choice of colours, of course.
4. Fill in the balls of yarn with rows of chain stitch and any of the colours you wish; lastly, fill the knitting needles with 666 and satin stitch.

Creative ideas

This is an ideal motif for people who enjoy crafts and might be used alongside the Sewing Machine (page 93) or the Artist's Palette (page 96).

Motif 70:
Pram

Whether you call it a pram, buggy or baby carriage, here's a useful motif for celebrating the birth of a new baby – and you can use traditional colours of pink and blue, or choose your own colour palette.

Thread colours

- 605 shell pink
- 3806 fuchsia
- 746 ivory
- 894 candy pink
- 310 black

Use two strands of thread throughout, unless otherwise stated.

1. With 605 and satin stitch, fill in all the small circles for the wheels, handle and near the heart.
2. Now using 3806, fill in the heart shape with split stitch filling. With the same colour, and using satin stitch, fill in the handle and the frame below the body.
3. With 746, fill in the lacy edge on the hood with satin stitch. Next, change to three strands of 894 and follow all the outlines on the body and hood with backstitch.
4. For the wheels, continuing with 894, stitch along the spokes using split stitch, then switch to 310 and work the tyres in satin stitch.

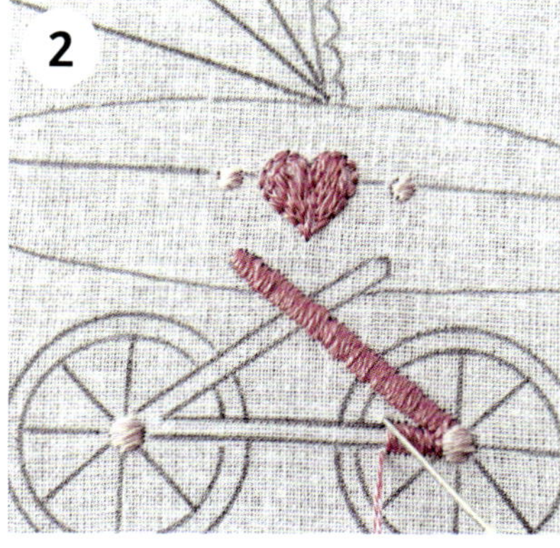

Notes on technique

You could fill in the larger shapes instead of outlining them – but if you are stitching this motif on an item for a baby, make sure you keep your stitches short or they could be snagged by tiny fingers.

Creative ideas

If you embroider this motif using mainly outlining stitches as shown in the example above, it is quick and simple enough for a birth congratulations card or even a batch of birth announcement cards or christening invitations.

Motif 71:
Artist's Palette

This palette motif, with its splodges of paint, makes an ideal pattern for the artist in your life – with or without the decorative foliage.

Thread colours

- 436 cappuccino
- 666 red
- 927 grey
- 741 tangerine
- 444 yellow
- 703 shamrock
- 3846 aqua
- 798 royal blue
- 208 violet
- 3609 heliotrope

Use two strands of thread throughout.

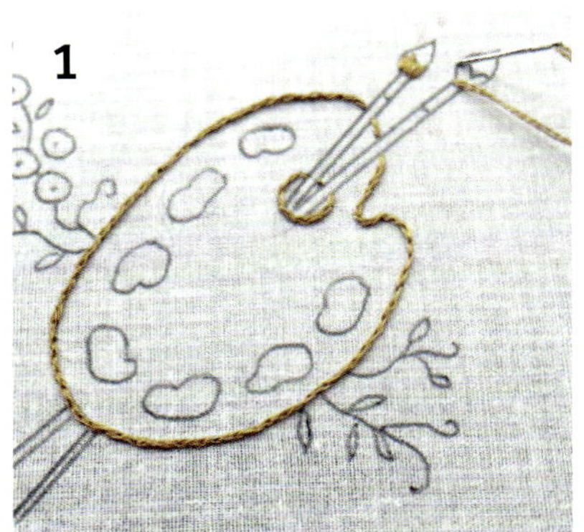

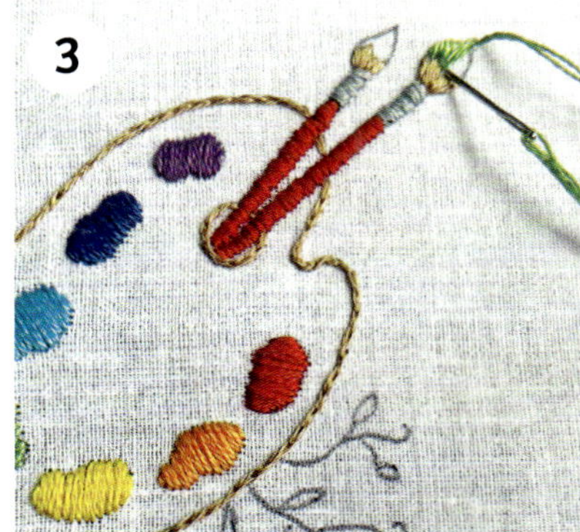

1. With 436, outline the palette in split stitch, including the thumb hole through which the paintbrushes emerge. Fill in the bristles on the brushes with satin stitch.
2. Continuing with satin stitch, fill in the brush handles with 666, except for the ferrules, which can be filled with 927. Don't forget to fill in the handles below the palette, too!
3. Now use 666, 741, 444, 703, 3846, 798 and 208 in satin stitch for the dabs of paint. Choose one or two colours from this selection to fill in the tips of the brushes.
4. Fill the flowers – the little circles – with 3609 and satin stitch, working the stitches from the outline to the centre. For the stems, use 703 and split stitch, and for each leaf a detached chain stitch filled with a single straight stitch.

Creative ideas

If you outline the palette rather than filling in the whole shape, it's relatively quick to complete, and you could scatter several identical palettes across the fabric.

Motif 72:
Party Decorations

This party cornucopia is exploding with confetti and streamers, making it the ideal motif for a special celebration.

Thread colours

- 444 yellow
- 307 buttermilk
- 907 lime
- 16 celery
- 798 royal blue
- 799 cornflower
- 666 red
- 741 tangerine

Use two strands of thread throughout.

1. Work the three streamers emerging from the cone in satin stitch. Use 444 and 307 for one, 907 and 16 for another, and 798 and 799 for the third, and in each case, use the darker shade for the sections at the front of the twist and the lighter shade for the inside areas.
2. Using 666, first outline the cone with split stitch, then fill in the stripes with satin stitch.
3. Now, using the colours used previously and 741, fill in the smaller streamers and larger shreds of confetti with satin stitch. Work French knots on each of the smaller pieces of confetti, indicated by dots.

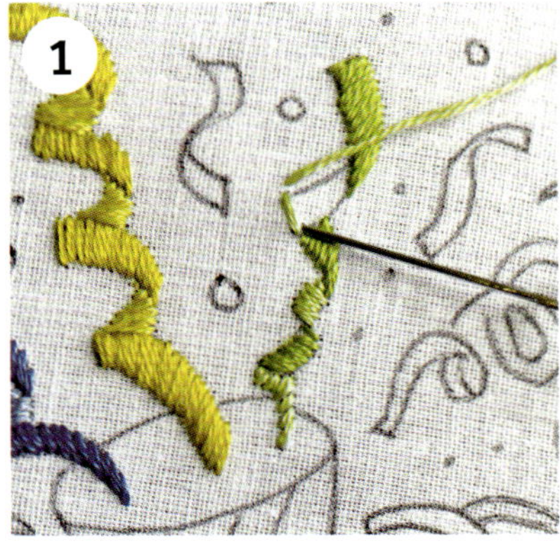

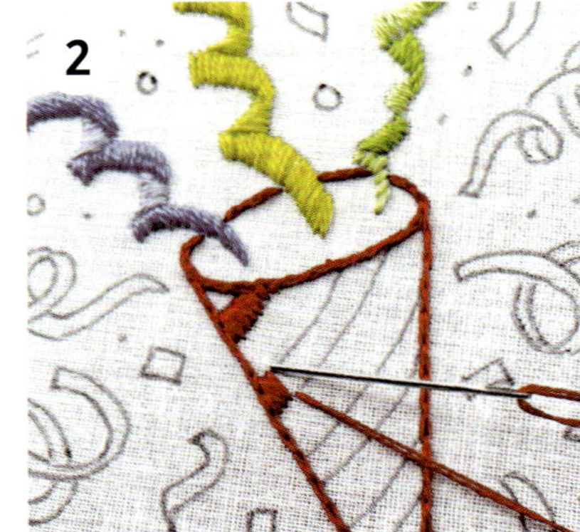

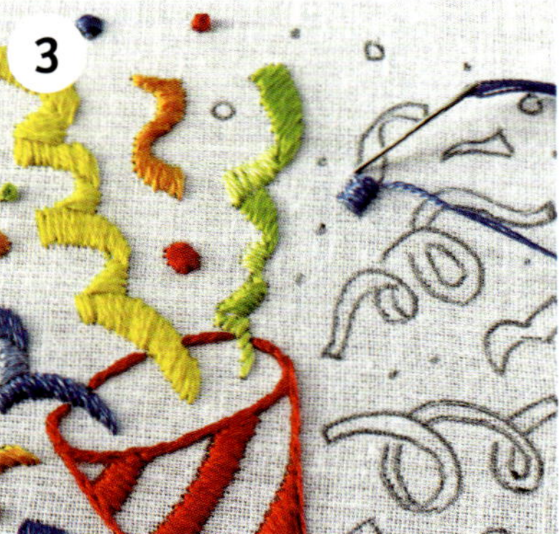

Creative ideas

This is, of course, an ideal motif for a party invitation. You could embroider it once, then photocopy the embroidery multiple times to make paper invitations.

Motif 73:
Cake

Here's a motif suitable for all kinds of celebrations. Keep the candle for birthdays, but for other occasions you may want to omit it or replace it with additional flowers.

Thread colours

- 800 sky blue
- 605 shell pink
- B5200 white
- 3806 fuchsia
- 307 buttermilk
- 642 stone
- 741 tangerine

Use two strands of thread throughout.

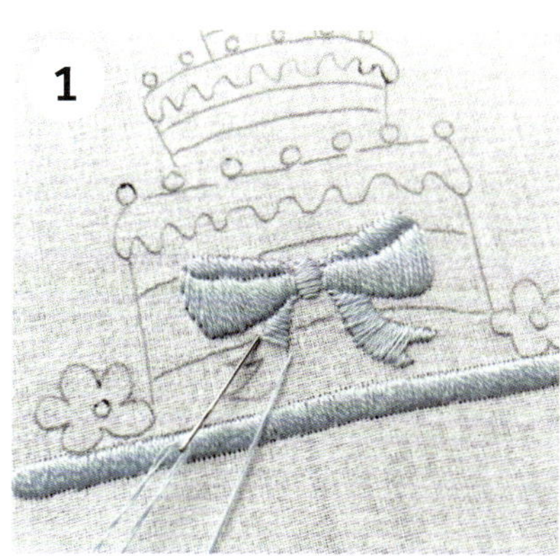

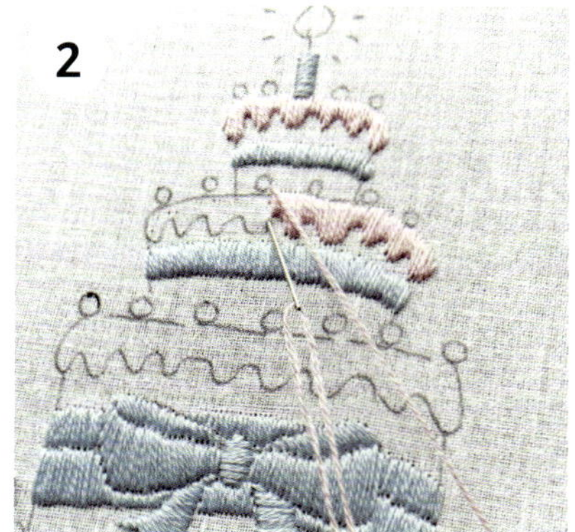

1. With 800, fill in the cake board, the bow, the candle and the ribbons in each layer with satin stitch.
2. Switch to 605 and fill in the layers of icing, once again using satin stitch. Next, fill in the areas of cake in between using B5200, leaving the spaces for the decorations unstitched.
3. Fill in the decorations using 3806, then fill in the flower petals with the same colour, all in satin stitch. Switch to 307 and fill in the flower centres, again with satin stitch.
4. To finish the candle, fill in the flame with 307 in satin stitch, then add a single straight stitch in 642 for the candle wick and work more single straight stitches in 741 for the lines depicting the candle glow, including in the centre of the flame.

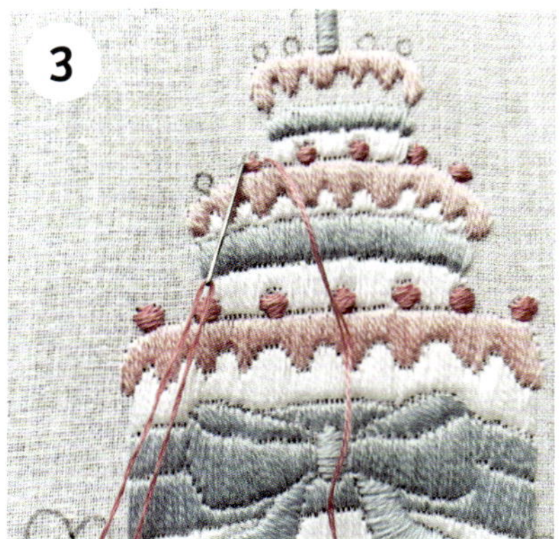

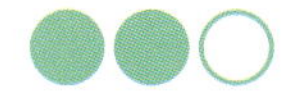

Motif 74: Fireplace

An old-fashioned fireplace with log fire and mantelpiece conjures up days gone by, before the arrival of central heating.

Thread colours

- 3810 sea green
- 988 sage
- 563 pistachio
- 645 dark grey
- 869 cocoa
- 444 yellow
- 742 apricot
- 740 orange

Use two strands of thread throughout.

1. Using satin stitch, fill in the three small circles on the fire surround with 3810 and the shapes immediately surrounding them with 988.
2. Continuing with satin stitch, fill in the three central panels of the fire surround with 563. For the border, use 988, except for the central scroll on the lower edge of the mantelpiece and the two rectangles at the base on either side, which you can fill with 3810.
3. Fill in the clock casing with 563 and 3810 in satin stitch, then work small straight stitches on the clock face using 645. Using the same thread colour, work satin stitch for the grate.
4. Again working in satin stitch, use 869 to fill in the logs and, working from the centre outwards, 444, 742 and 740 for the flames.

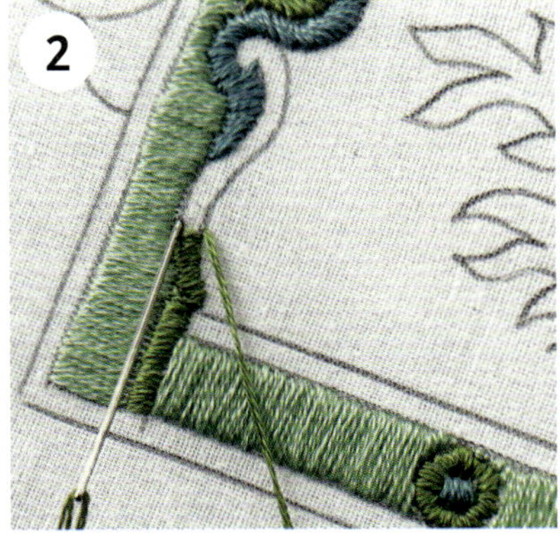

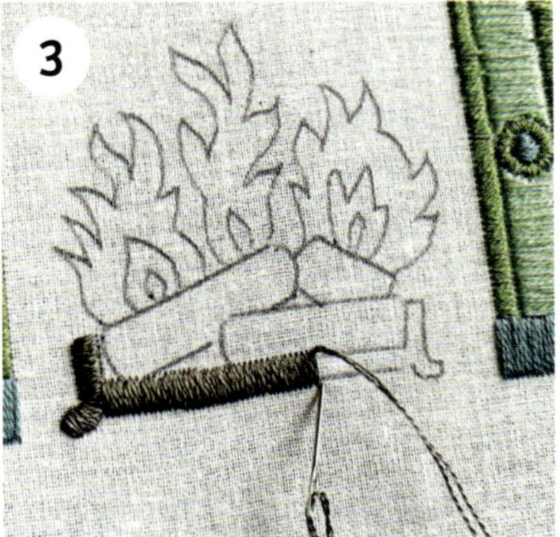

Creative ideas

This would make a good choice for a card to welcome someone to their new home. For a Christmas card, you could add a couple of stockings hanging from the mantelpiece.

Motif 75:
Truck

Here's a truck making a delivery – which could be two Christmas trees. It's up to you how you choose to interpret it.

Thread colours

- 799 cornflower
- 798 royal blue
- 927 grey
- 310 black
- 307 buttermilk
- 666 red
- 436 cappuccino
- 703 shamrock

Use two strands of thread throughout.

1. Fill in the main sections of the truck's body with 799 and satin stitch, then highlight the central horizontal lines and the side rail in 798 and backstitch and satin stitch, respectively.
2. Fill in the bumpers – or fenders – as well as the door handles and hub caps in 927, using satin stitch, then fill in the tyres in 310 with satin stitches radiating out from the centres to the rims.
3. Fill in the headlight in 307 and add a couple of satin stitches in 666 to the back of the truck to represent the tail light.
4. Use 436 and satin stitch to fill in the tree trunk, then use 703 and split stitch filling for the foliage. Finally, follow the outlines of the hills with split stitch and the lines in the road with backstitch, using 436.

Notes on technique

Satin stitch is good for filling small shapes, whether regular, like the mostly rectangular shapes that make up the truck, or irregular. Make sure the stitch length is kept short: divide large shapes into smaller ones where necessary.

Creative ideas

You could combine this motif with others such as the Cars (page 103) or Caravan (page 105).

Motif 76:
Place Setting

Use this design for all kinds of applications and to convey various messages from invitations, congratulations or declarations of love.

Thread colours

- 703 shamrock
- 3806 fuchsia
- 322 French blue
- 927 grey

Use two strands of thread throughout.

1. Using 703, embroider the stems and leaves with stem stitch and satin stitch, respectively. Fill in the sections of flower petals using satin stitch and 3806.
2. Outline the plate with split stitch and 322. Use the same colour and satin stitch for the cutlery handles.
3. Now use 927 in satin stitch for the metal parts. Fill in the bowl of the spoon in two stages – an oval centre and a border surrounding it, with stitches fanning outwards slightly to accommodate the curved shape.

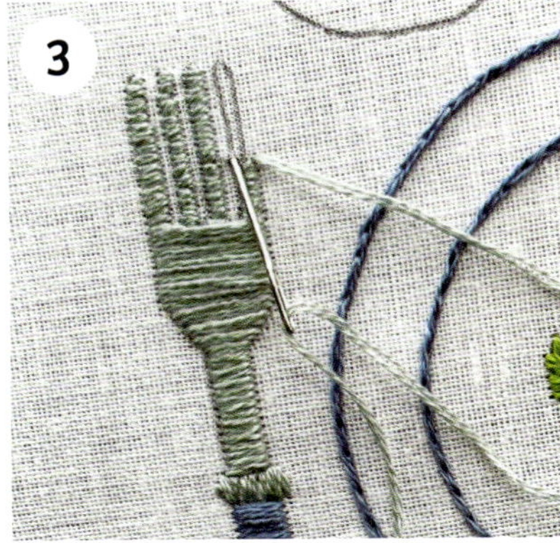

Creative ideas

This would make a good choice for a greetings card, as an invitation to a dinner party or as a Valentine. You could also use this motif on a set of napkins, perhaps adding someone's initial to each.

Motif 77: Teapot

This simple motif is one of the quickest and easiest to embroider, especially if you stick to simple outlining stitches.

Thread colours

- 645 dark grey
- 943 pine green
- 340 lavender
- 307 buttermilk

Use one strand of thread throughout, unless otherwise stated.

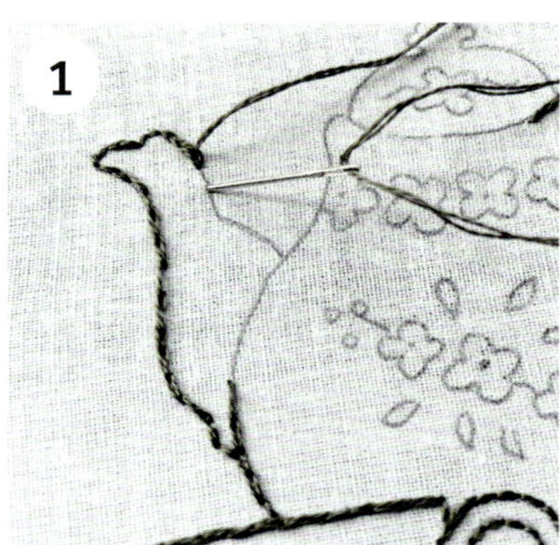

1. Outline the teapot, cup and saucer in split stitch, using two strands of 645.
2. For the flower decoration, use one strand of 943 and split stitch for the stems; then satin stitch for the leaves. Use one strand of 340 and satin stitch the flowers and buds.
3. Finally, add a French knot in the centre of each flower, using one strand of 307.

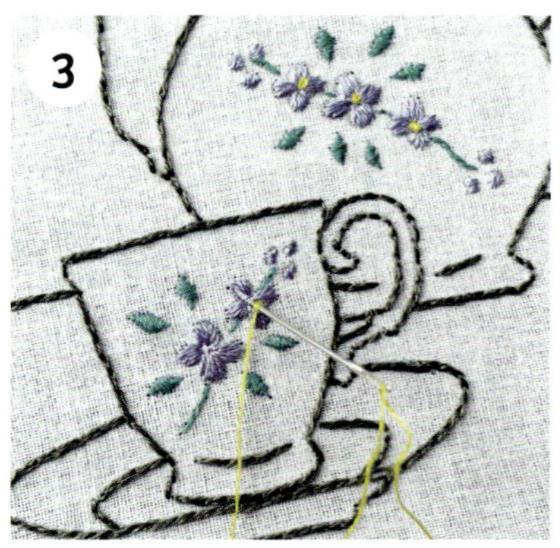

Creative ideas

The most obvious application for this motif is as a decoration on a tea cosy, where you could add further embellishments with a floral border.

Motif 78:
Cars

Here are three different cars, sure to appeal to children who love toy cars and to grown-ups who prefer the real thing.

Thread colours

- 988 sage
- 798 royal blue
- 666 red
- 927 grey
- 307 buttermilk
- B5200 white
- 310 black

Use two strands of thread throughout.

1. For the bodywork of each car, fill it in, section by section, in satin stitch. For this example, 988 has been used for the top car, 798 for the middle car and 666 for the bottom car.
2. Use 927 for the bumpers (fenders), door handles and hubcaps (wheel covers), for the latter working for the outside to the centre.
3. Continuing with satin stitch, use 307 for the headlights and 666 or B5200 for the rear lights. Finally, use 310 for the tyres.

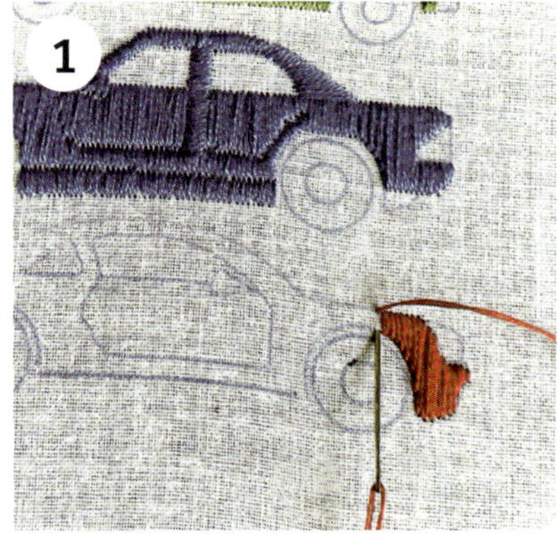

Creative ideas

Three cars stacked on top of one another fits well into the square format used for all the motifs in this book. However, separating them out as individual cars, scattered across a background, makes a great repeat pattern for a cushion or throw. They could also be arranged in a row and it's easy to change the direction of the centre car so that they are all facing the same way.

Motif 79:
Bicycle

The word 'bicycle' simply means two wheels – and these simple two-wheeled vehicles are the most efficient way for human beings to convert energy into mobility.

Thread colours

- 800 sky blue
- 645 dark grey
- 322 French blue
- 703 shamrock
- 3806 fuchsia

Use two strands of thread throughout.

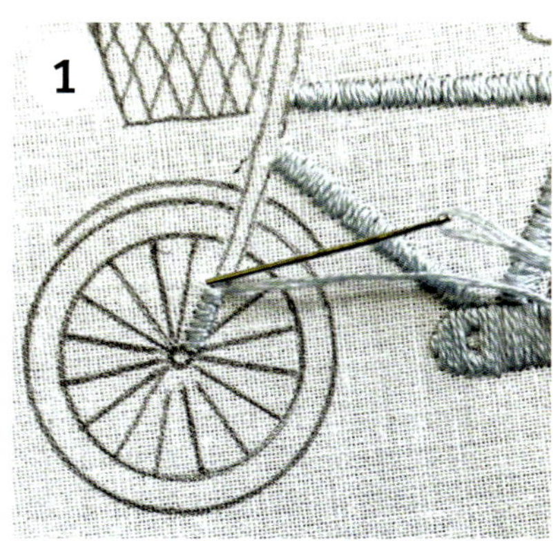

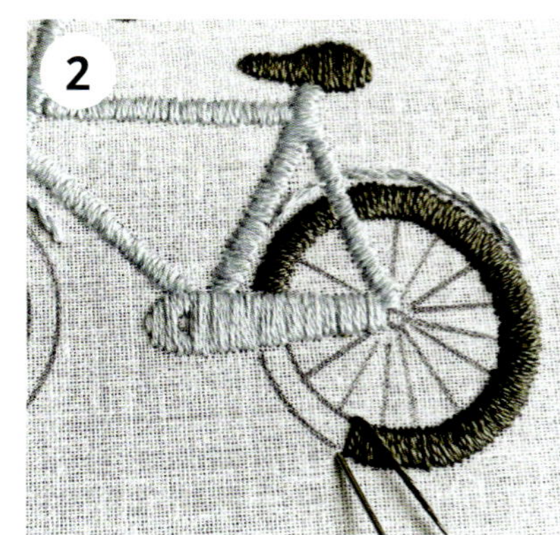

1. Using 800, fill in the frame of the bike, including the chain guard, with satin stitch, then fill in the mudguards in stem stitch.
2. Switch to 645 and work satin stitch for the saddle, handlebars and tyres. Change to 322 and split stitch for the wheel spokes.
3. Still using 322, work split stitches for the basket. Finally, embroider the flowers using 703 and stem stitch for the stems and leaves, and 3806 and satin stitch for the flower heads.

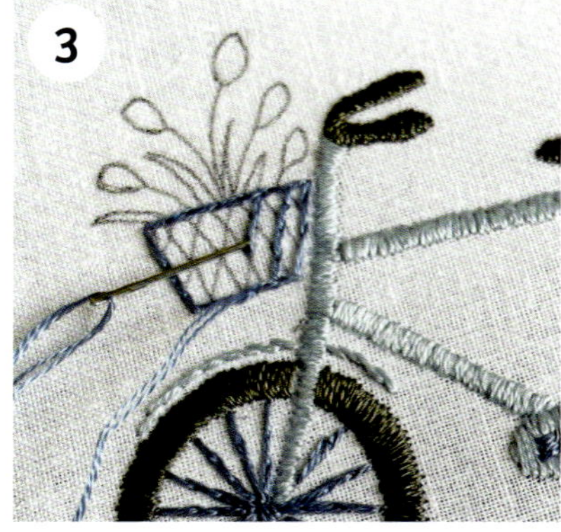

Creative ideas

There are several motifs in the book that this could be used alongside, such as the Cars (page 103) and Truck (page 100), perhaps to decorate a book cover or bag.

Motif 80:
Caravan

Some people live in caravans – or mobile homes – while some just tow one behind their car for a home-from-home holiday.

Thread colours

- 335 pomegranate
- 760 salmon
- 800 sky blue
- 642 stone
- 444 yellow
- 840 sepia
- 608 flame
- 703 shamrock

Use two strands of thread throughout.

1. Working in satin stitch, start by filling in the heart shape on the door using 335. For the curtains and the door use 760. Next, for the stripe across the centre of the caravan and the tops of the windows, use 800.
2. Now outline the main shape of the caravan and the windows using 642 and backstitch. With the same colour, fill in the doorstep and wheel with satin stitch. Work a French knot in the centre of the wheel, using 444.
3. Fill in the tree trunks with satin stitch and 840, adjusting the directions or length of the stitch for the cut ends, as needed.
4. With 642, stitch along the string of the bunting with split stitch, then fill in the bunting pennants with satin stitch using 608, 444, 703, 800 and 335.
5. Finally, using 703, stitch the horizontal line for the horizon and the tufts of grass at the base of the posts with split stitch.

Creative ideas

This is a good companion piece for the Truck (page 100) and Cars (page 103). You can place them in a row to create a decorative border for a child's bedcover.

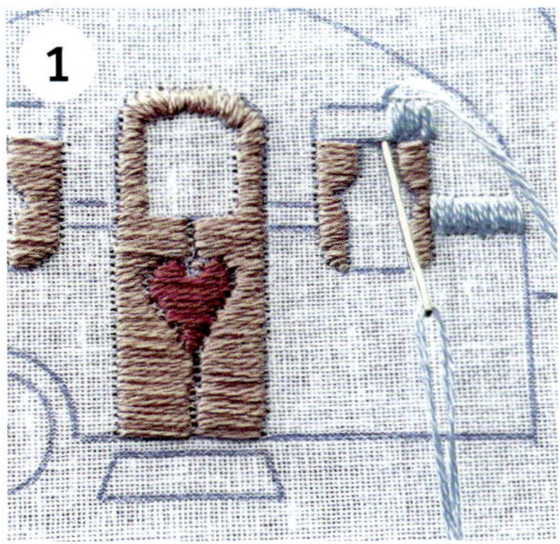

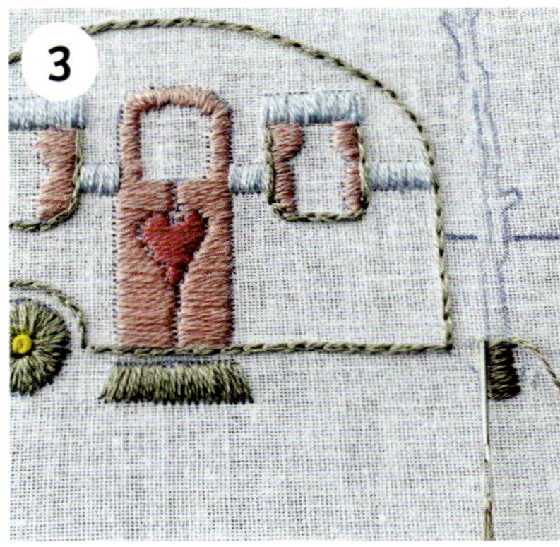

Motif 81:
Mermaid

With the head and body of a human and the tail of a fish, the mermaid is a favourite mythical creature and features in numerous fairy tales and popular movies.

Thread colours

- 353 blush
- 645 dark grey
- 891 watermelon
- 608 flame
- 563 pistachio
- 943 pine green
- 3810 sea green
- 3846 aqua
- 995 turquoise
- 340 lavender
- 3341 peach

Use two strands of thread throughout, unless otherwise stated.

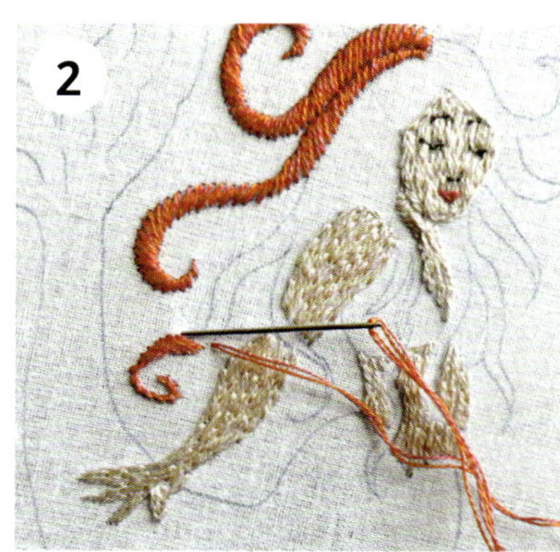

1. Fill in the face and other areas of skin in the arm and abdomen using split stitch filling and 353. Switch to a single strand of 645 to embroider the nose, eyes and eyebrows in split stitches, then work the mouth in 891.
2. Thread the needle with one strand each of 891 and 608 and fill in the strands of hair using satin stitch. Fill in the bra with 563 and satin stitch.
3. Still using 563, start filling in the tail from the waist down with chain stitch, working the rows across the width of the tail. After a few rows, change to one strand of 563 and one strand of 943 combined. After a few more rows, use 943 alone.
4. Keep changing threads in this way after every several rows: use 943 with 3810, followed by 3810 alone; use 3810 and 3846, followed by 3846 alone; and finally use 3846 and 995, which should take you as far as the base of the tail fluke.
5. Embroider the fluke with 340 for the interior lines and 995 to fill, working the rows of chain stitch along the length of the two sides.
6. Fill in the starfish and seaweed in satin stitch, using 3341 for the starfish, and adding a few French knots, and 943 for the seaweed.

Motif 82: Dragon

The dragon is a legendary creature that appears in cultural folklore around the world. Whether they are good or evil, they symbolize supernatural power and strength.

Thread colours

- 608 flame
- 347 russet
- 666 red
- 645 dark grey

Use two strands of thread throughout.

1. Beginning at the tip of the snout and using two strands of 608, outline the top of the head and back of the neck in split stitch. Now work the wing in blanket stitch, then continue along both sides of the tail in split stitch and finish at the top of the hind legs.
2. Still using split stitch, change to 347 to outline the underside of the chin and the two legs that are at the back, then complete the outline, apart from the tongue, and the internal lines to give shape with 666.
3. Fill in the claws with satin stitch and 645, then outline the eye. Finally, fill in the tongue with satin stitch and using 608.

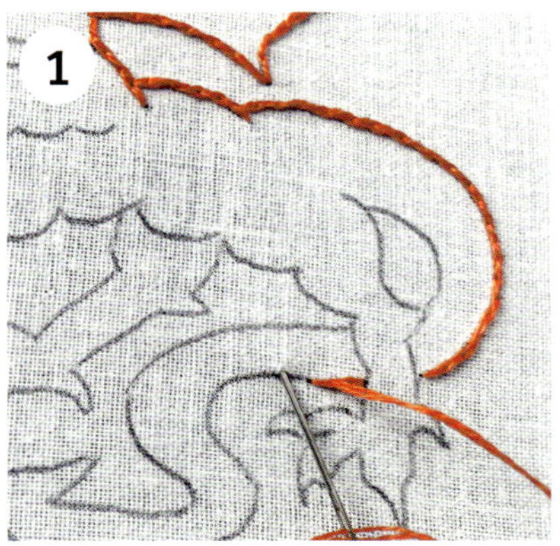

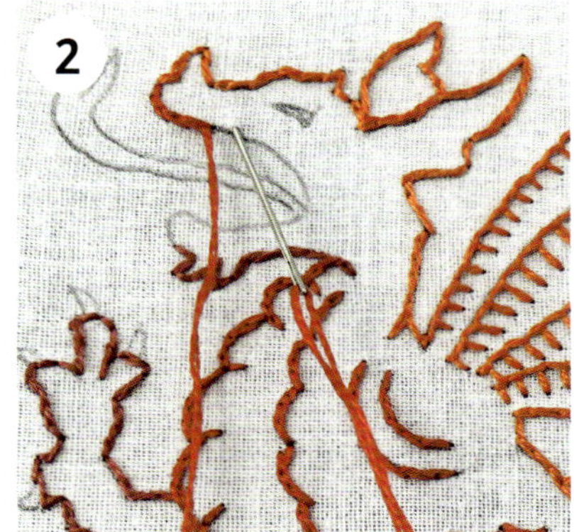

Motif 83:
Unicorn

The idea of this mythical beast, resembling a magical horse with a single horn, dates back to ancient Greece, but it remains popular in modern times as a cuddly toy and a decoration on children's clothing.

Thread colours

- B5200 white
- 3042 heather
- 340 lavender
- 894 candy pink
- 800 sky blue
- 3609 heliotrope
- 645 dark grey

Use two strands of thread throughout.

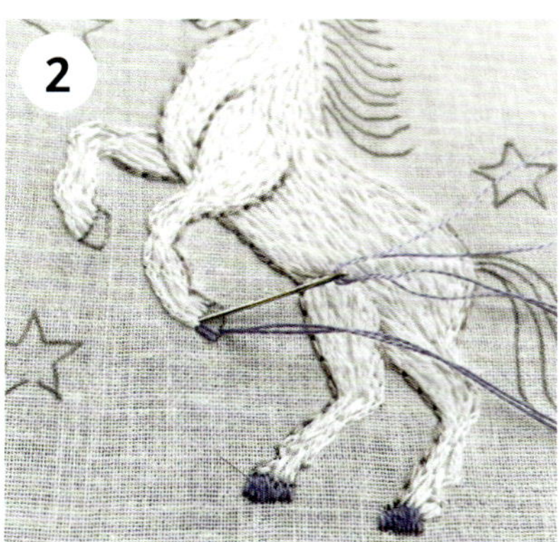

1. Fill in the whole body, including the ears, with split stitch filling in B5200, leaving the horn, tail, mane and hooves unstitched.
2. Using 3042, outline some areas with backstitch to give definition such as the chest and under the belly and the insides of the legs. Using 340, fill in the hooves and horn with satin stitch.
3. For the mane and tail, use 894, 800 and 3609 to stitch individual strands in split stitch, creating a multicoloured effect.
4. Fill in the stars with the same three colours as the mane, using satin stitch. Use 645 to define the eye.

Creative ideas

What colour is a unicorn's horn? And its tail? Its hooves? Because it's a fantasy creature there is no answer to these questions, so you can use your imagination and creativity. You could, of course, use shimmering threads and even add a sprinkling of glittery sequins to your embroidery.

Notes on technique

Adding an outline to a few selected areas can help to make a motif stand out, especially where it is worked in a similar colour to the background fabric.

Motif 84:
Masks

Symbolic of the theatre, the dramatic masks of tragedy and comedy suggest other types of entertainment, too, such as carnivals and masked balls.

Thread colours

- 553 grape
- 3607 red-violet
- 3806 fuchsia
- 894 candy pink

Use two strands of thread throughout, unless otherwise stated.

1. Keeping stitches short, neat and even, outline the masks in backstitch using three strands of 553.
2. Now change to two strands of 553 and outline the noses and eyebrows with split stitch and fill in the mouths and eyes with satin stitch.
3. For the streamers, work in satin stitch for the wider parts and stem stitch for the narrower lines, using 3607, 3806 and 894.

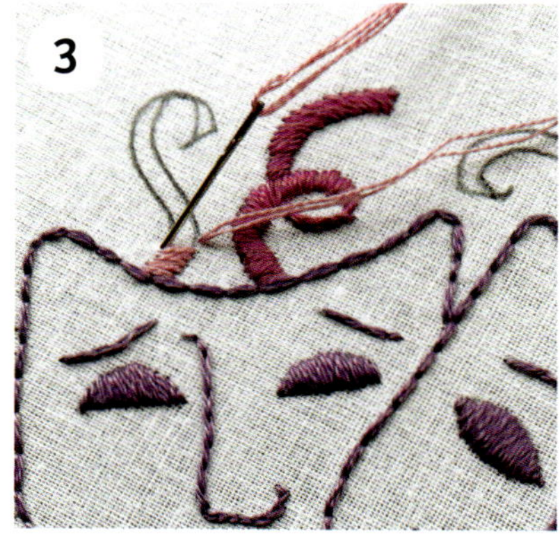

Creative ideas

A harmonious palette of closely related colours has been used in this motif, but remember that it is just a suggestion of how you might stitch it. You could just as easily choose bright, contrasting colours instead, depending on the mood you wish to create.

Motif 85:
Dream Catcher

Representing positive energy, the dream catcher is a symbol of Native American spirituality and is believed to protect sleepers from bad dreams.

Thread colours

- 746 ivory
- 3046 beige
- 3846 aqua
- 642 stone
- 3042 heather
- 436 cappuccino

Use two strands of thread throughout, unless otherwise stated.

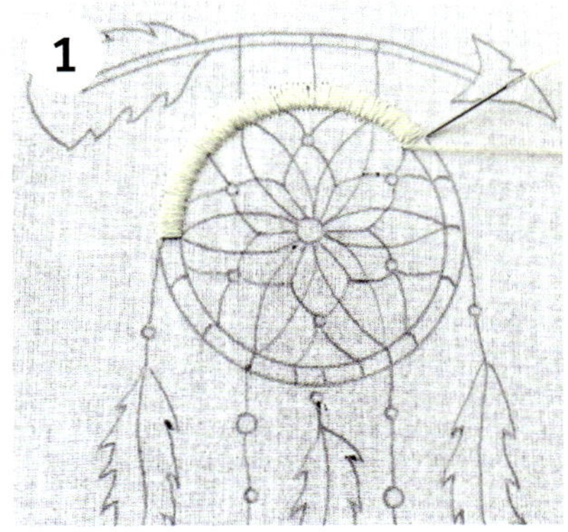

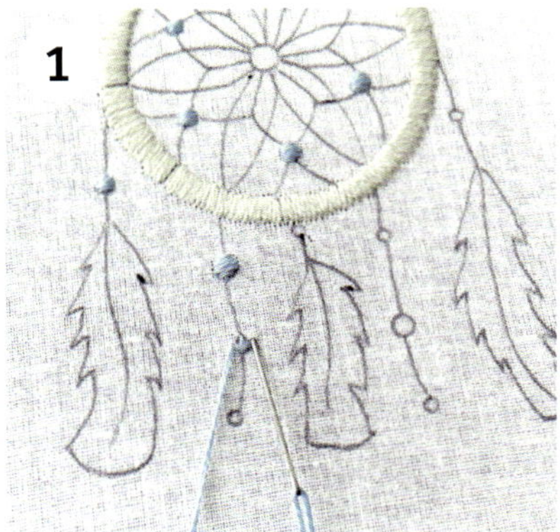

1. Using 746 and satin stitch, embroider the ring. Switch to 3046 to work satin stitch for the arrow shaft, then fill in each bead with satin stitch, using 3846.
2. Now, using a single strand of 642 and split stitch, follow the web of lines to form the pattern within and attached to the circle, as well as those attaching the ring to the arrow and dangling feathers and beads. (Where the lines are covered by satin stitch, refer to the main artwork.)
3. Use two strands of 642 and satin stitch to fill in the arrow head, then fill in the main part of the feather on the arrow with 746 and the tip with 642. Work these satin stitches on a diagonal slope from the edge towards the centre.
4. Continue these diagonal satin stitches for the other feathers, using one strand of 746 and one strand of 3046 for the main part and either 3042, 3046 or 436 for the tips. Finish by embroidering the central quill in 746, using split stitch.

Notes on technique

You will need to draw very fine or erasable lines on the fabric, otherwise they will not be covered when stitching with a single strand of thread.

Motif 86:
Heart

A heart is a useful motif for all kinds of occasions and applications. This one is inspired by Mexican folk art and offers plenty of scope for creative stitching.

Thread colours

- 666 red
- 3806 fuchsia
- 943 pine green
- 444 yellow
- 3607 red-violet
- 799 cornflower

Use two strands of thread throughout, unless otherwise stated.

1. Using 666, fill in the central heart shape with split stitch filling. Switch to 3806, then work blanket stitch all round, working across the width of the space between the edge of the central heart and the neighbouring outline.
2. Fill in the next shape with 943 and split stitch filling to form a wide border.
3. Now use 444 and satin stitch to fill in the small diamond above the large heart, then change to 666 and fill in all the small heart shapes using split stitch filling.
4. Fill in the remaining shapes using satin stitch and 3806, 3607, 444 and 799.

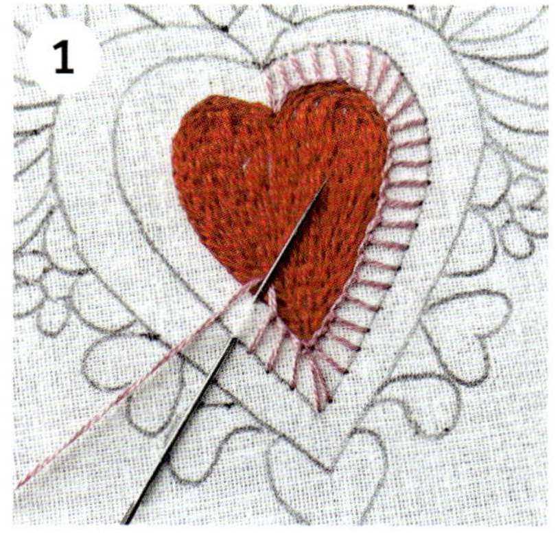

Creative ideas

There are so many things you could do with this motif. Richly stitched, like the sample shown here, it would look particularly good embroidered on a jacket or other garment.

Motif 87:
Banner

Inspired by a classic tattoo design, this pretty motif features a bird, a floral swag and a customizable banner.

Thread colours

- B5200 white
- 307 buttermilk
- 800 sky blue
- 799 cornflower
- 798 royal blue
- 891 watermelon
- 703 shamrock
- 894 candy pink

Use two strands of thread throughout.

1. Fill in the banner using B5200 and split stitch filling, then fill in the eye with satin stitch. Change to 307 and fill in the beak and the flower centres.
2. Now fill in the top of the bird's body with split stitch shading. Start along the top edge, threading the needle with one strand of B5200 and one strand of 800. As you go down the shape, every two or three rows, change colour, first to two strands of 800, followed by one strand each of 800 and 799, then two strands of 799, followed by one strand each of 799 and 798.
3. Use split stitch filling and 798 alone for the centre section, above the wing, and 799 for the centre front section. For the breast of the bird, change to 891, for a pretty contrast.
4. Fill in the wings in a similar way to the body, then fill in the wing feathers and tail in satin stitch, using 799.
5. For the flowers, using 703, follow the line of the stems in split stitch and fill in the leaves in satin stitch. Now switch to 894 and satin stitch to fill in the flower petals, working the stitches across the shapes.
6. For the largest flower, work a few straight stitches on the petals in 891, radiating outwards from the centre.

Creative ideas

In the example shown here, the banner has been filled with split stitch, but you could instead outline it and add a message within, such as a birthday greeting or a name and date.

Motif 88: Stars

Throughout the ages, twinkling stars have fascinated night-sky gazers around the world, but you won't need to stay up late to admire these stars.

Thread colours

- 444 yellow
- 800 sky blue

Use two strands of thread throughout.

1. Start by dividing each of the larger star shapes into equal segments, then fill in each diamond-shaped piece using satin stitch and 444, arranging the stitches across the shapes.
2. For the smaller stars it's easier and more effective to work the satin stitches from the outline towards the centre.
3. Change to 800 and stitch along the swirly lines with chain stitch. Finish the final swirly line with French knots in 444.

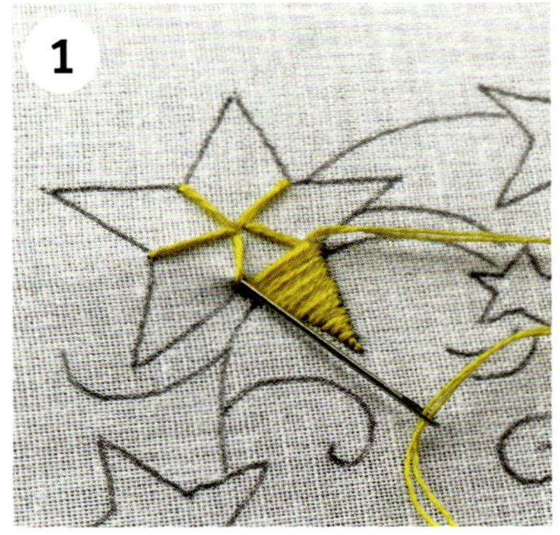

Notes on technique

If you are filling in the stars with satin stitch, it helps to divide the shape into five separate segments, as described above. You can do this by drawing lines with marker pen or you can use thread and straight stitches, whichever you find easier.

Motif 89:
Floral Border

Designed for personalization, you can add your choice of initials, name or message in the central space of this pretty botanical border.

Thread colours

- 703 shamrock
- 444 yellow
- 760 salmon
- 335 pomegranate

Use two strands of thread throughout.

1. Start by embroidering all the stems in stem stitch and the leaves in satin stitch, using 703.
2. With satin stitch, fill in the flower centres in 444 and the petals in 760. Now embroider a French knot on each small dot, using 335.
3. To add something to personalize the motif, trace it in the space in the centre of the wreath, using either a permanent or an erasable marker.
4. Here, a simple monogram is embroidered in 335, using stem stitch for the fine lines and satin stitch for the thicker parts of the lettering.

Creative ideas

Simply trace your choice of name or message in the space. You can design this yourself, by hand – or you can generate lettering using a computer, or find something appropriate in a book or magazine.

Motif 90:
Circus Tent

Also known as the big top, this colourful landmark is symbolic of the circus and all its associated fun and entertainment.

Thread colours

- 444 yellow
- 799 cornflower
- 645 dark grey
- 666 red
- B5200 white

Use two strands of thread throughout.

1. Working in satin stitch, fill in the swags across the centre of the tent using 444 and 799. Using 645, fill in the entrance and the five balls. Fill in the curtains by the entrance with 799 and the tie-backs with 444.
2. Now, continuing with satin stitch, fill in the stripes with 666 and B5200.
3. For the flag poles, use 645 and overcast stitch and, finally for the flags, return to satin stitch and use 799 and 666.

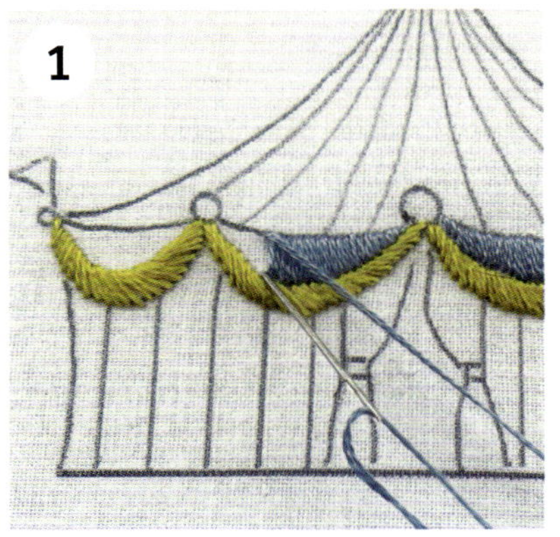

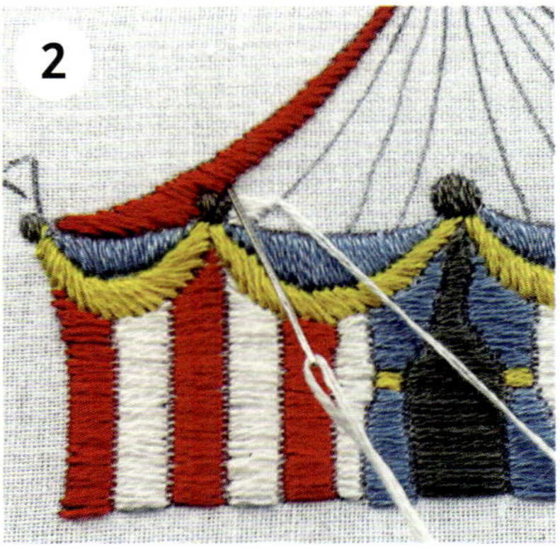

Creative ideas

This motif could be teamed with the Truck (page 100) and Caravan (page 105) to create a small scene to decorate a cushion cover or souvenir album.

Motif 91:
Paisley

This teardrop-shaped motif, known as a boteh or buta, is a characteristic component of traditional Persian paisley designs.

Thread colours

- 666 red
- 740 orange
- 3607 red-violet
- 208 violet
- 995 turquoise

Use two strands of thread throughout, unless otherwise stated.

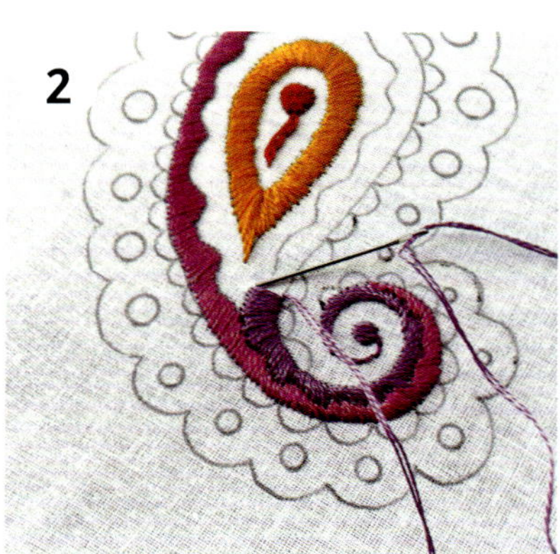

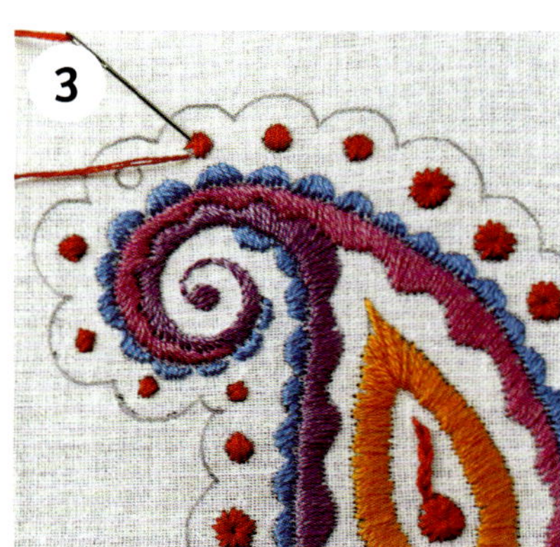

1. Start in the centre and work outwards. With 666, fill in the centre circle with satin stitch, bringing the needle out on the outline and down through the centre. Embroider the tail with chain stitch. Switch to 740 and, leaving an unstitched section, fill in the next teardrop shape with satin stitch.
2. Again, leave a section unstitched and fill in the shape with the wavy edge with satin stitch, using 3607 for one half and 208 for the other; change to backstitch at the narrow end and fill in the circle with satin stitch.
3. Fill in the scalloped border with 995 and satin stitch. Then switch back to 666 and fill in the large circles in a similar way to the central circle, but fill in the smaller ones with satin stitches running across the shapes.
4. For the outline, use three strands of 995 and backstitch, keeping the stitches small.

Creative ideas

Use one motif as a central decoration on a patchwork square, or repeat the motif as an all-over design on a larger piece, stitching each one with the same colours or with different colours for a rainbow effect.

Motif 92:
Globe

A terrestrial globe is a spherical model of the Earth – like a world map printed on a ball. The word 'globe' comes from the Latin globus, meaning sphere.

Thread colours

- 703 shamrock
- 3846 aqua
- 800 sky blue
- 742 apricot
- 3046 beige

Use two strands of thread throughout.

1. Fill in all of the land masses with 703, using split stitch filling, then outline each shape with split stitch and 3846.
2. Now fill in the rest of the circle with split stitch filling and 800, working the stitches from the unworked outer edges and smoothly adjusting to the land masses.
3. Using satin stitch, fill in the stand. For the curved support, use 742 and then for the attachments use 3046. For the stand, use 3046 and satin stitch.

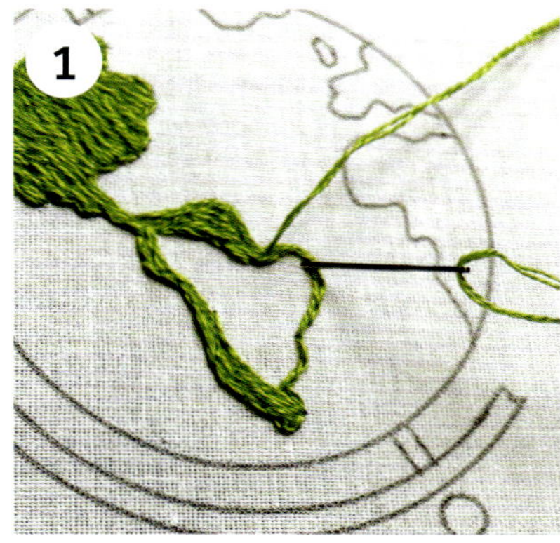

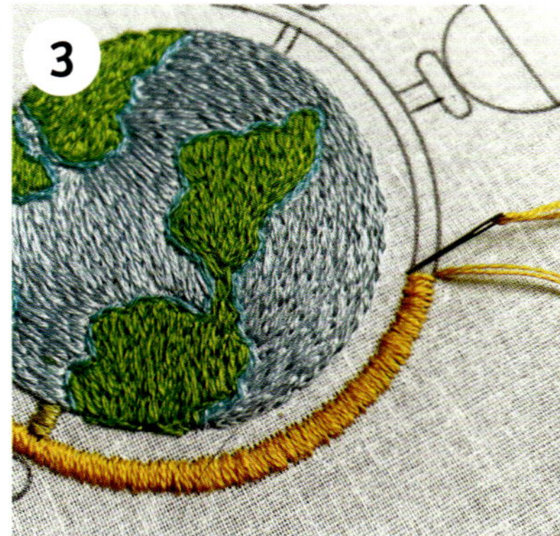

Creative ideas

This motif would be suitable for making a gift for a world traveller, such as a passport sleeve, a notebook cover or luggage label.

Motif 93:
Celtic Knot

If you look carefully, you will see that the interlocking shapes are composed of one continuous line. This is said to represent the endless cycle of life, death and rebirth.

Thread colours

- 335 pomegranate
- 740 orange
- 742 apricot
- 307 buttermilk
- 907 lime
- 3846 aqua
- 799 cornflower
- 340 lavender
- 3607 red-violet

Use three strands of thread throughout.

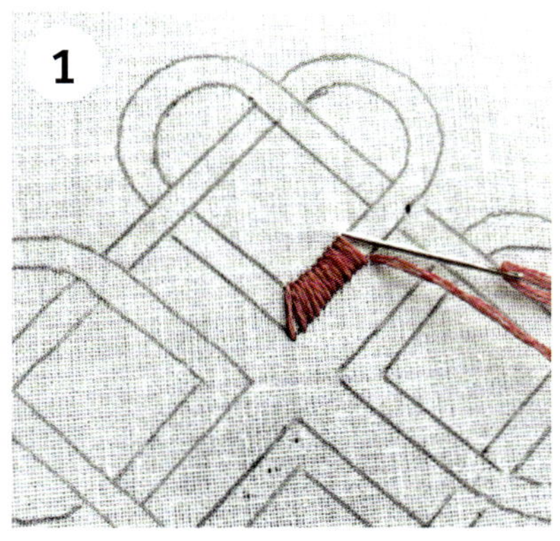

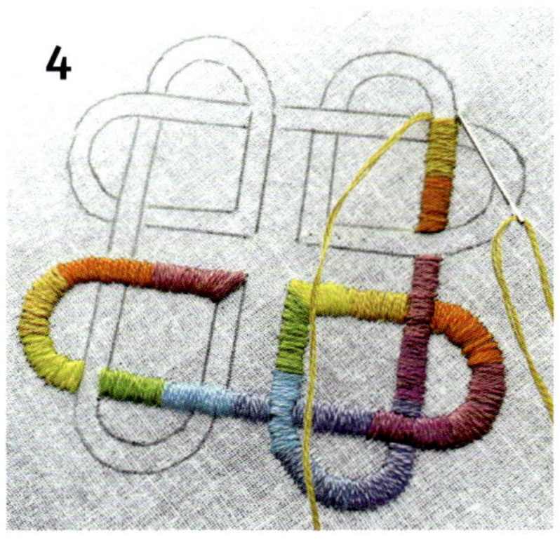

1. Starting at one of the points near the centre and using three strands of 335, work in satin stitch. Take the first stitch diagonally across the point, then gradually reduce the slant for the next few stitches until the stitches run across the width at right angles.
2. After about ½in (8–12mm), change to 740. As you reach the curve, make the stitches fan out slightly so they continue to run across the width.
3. Change again, this time to 742, then every ½in (8–12mm) change the threads in the following sequence: 307, 907, 3846, 799, 340 and 3607. When you reach a point where the lines intersect, leave a gap if the line goes underneath or carry on if the line is on top.
4. Start again with 335 and continue with the previous sequence until you reach the starting point.

Creative ideas

In this example, a spectrum of colours creates a rainbow effect. You could try other colour blends, shades of one colour, or simply embroider the whole shape in a single colour.

Motif 94:
Fan

Fans date back thousands of years – and even today a fan is a simple (non-technical) method for keeping cool on a hot day.

Thread colours

- 746 ivory
- 563 pistachio
- 553 grape
- 340 lavender
- 741 tangerine

Use two strands of thread throughout.

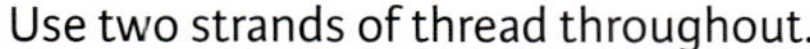

1. Fill in the two flowers with 746 and satin stitch, working each petal individually and in two halves, with the stitches sloping downwards. Fill in the leaves with 563, still using satin stitch.
2. Now fill in the fan with split stitch filling, using 553 and 340 on alternate segments.
3. Fill in the ribbons with 563 and satin stitch, slanting the stitches.
4. Finally, add stamens to the flowers with 741, using single straight stitches and French knots.

Notes on technique

When you fill in the flower petals, you will cover up some of the drawn lines, so when it comes to adding the stamens you will have to do this freehand. Just refer to the original artwork for guidance, or use your own creativity.

Motif 95:
Mandala

A mandala is a circular geometric design that is, in Hindu and Buddhist cultures, extremely symbolic. Mandalas have become popular in Western cultures in recent years as printed designs to colour in to improve mindfulness.

Thread colours

- 608 flame
- 991 jade
- 16 celery
- 3806 fuchsia

Use two strands of thread throughout, unless otherwise stated.

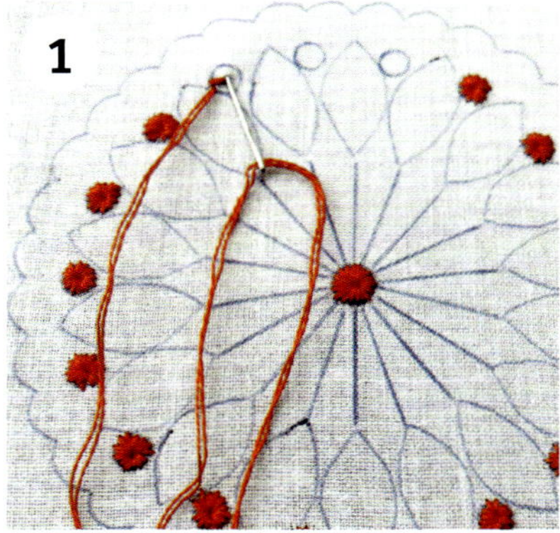

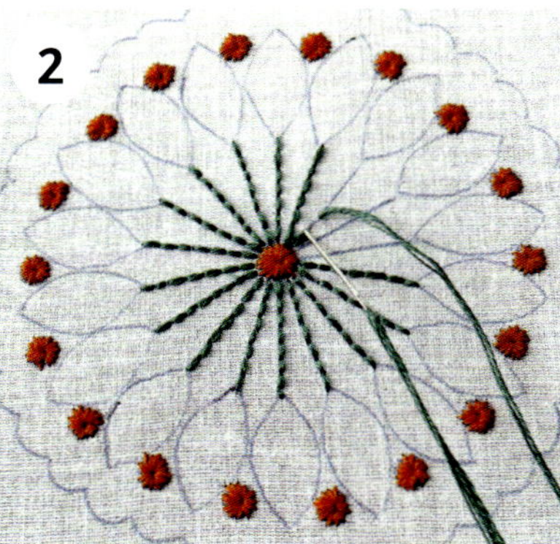

1. Fill in each small circle with satin stitch in 608, with the stitches radiating out from the centre.
2. With three strands of 991, stitch along the straight lines with backstitch. Fill in all the petal shapes with 16 and satin stitch, working the stitches across the width of each shape.
3. Switch to 3806 and embroider the outline in buttonhole stitch, keeping the stitches even and close together.

Creative ideas

This embroidery motif demonstrates that mandalas are not just for colouring books but can provide interesting textile designs, too.

Notes on technique

The border of closely made buttonhole stitch allows you to cut out the motif, if you wish to use it as a patch or appliqué.

Motif 96:
Crown

A crown is a circular ornament made from precious metals and adorned with jewels, usually worn by a monarch, so it has great significance.

Thread colours

- 666 red
- 701 emerald green
- 799 cornflower
- B5200 white
- 3046 beige
- 742 apricot
- 783 mustard
- 208 violet

Use two strands of thread throughout.

1. Fill in the jewels – rubies, emeralds, sapphires and diamonds – using 666, 701, 799 and B5200 with satin stitch.
2. Continuing with satin stitch, fill in the settings for the large stones and the fan-shaped decorations using 3046, then fill in the lower border and the arches of the crown using 742.
3. With 783, fill in the band, dividing it into two sections so the stitches won't be too wide.
4. Using 208 and split stitch filling, fill in the fabric part – the cap – working smaller stitches around the outlines of the jewels.

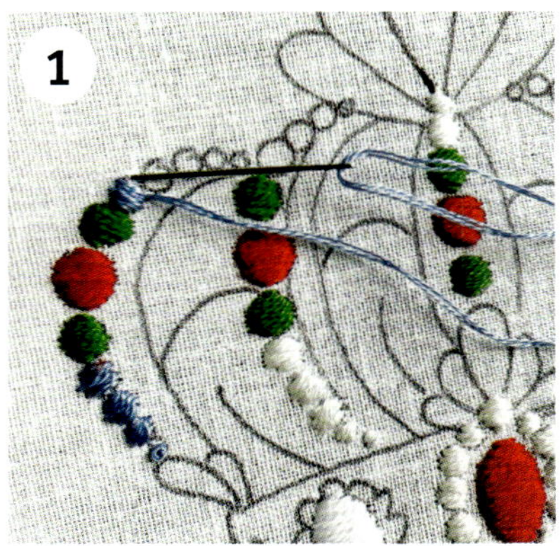

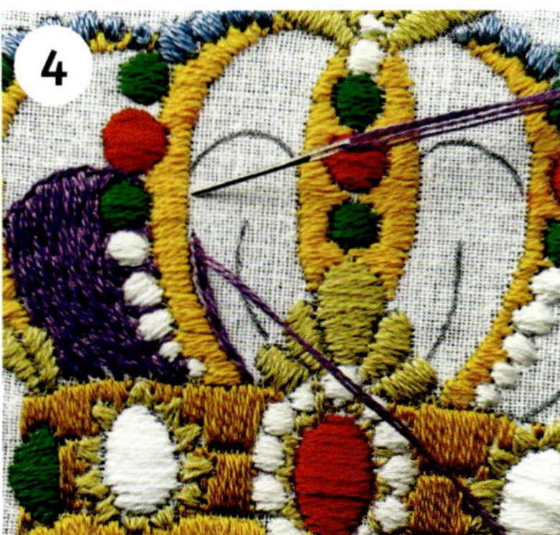

Creative ideas

You don't have to create such a colourful crown: instead of a multitude of jewels, use ivory thread to transform the embellishments into pearls of various sizes.

Motif 97:
Rainbow

Most people are delighted when a rainbow – a multicoloured arc of light – appears in the sky. It has such a magical quality.

Thread colours

- B5200 white
- 553 grape
- 798 royal blue
- 3846 aqua
- 702 fern
- 444 yellow
- 741 tangerine
- 891 watermelon

Use two strands of thread throughout.

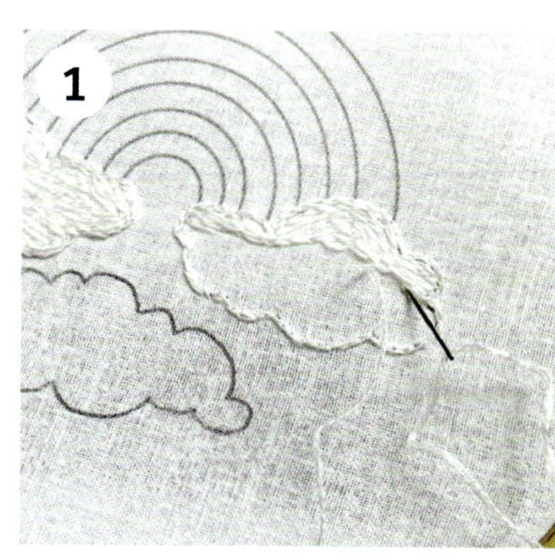

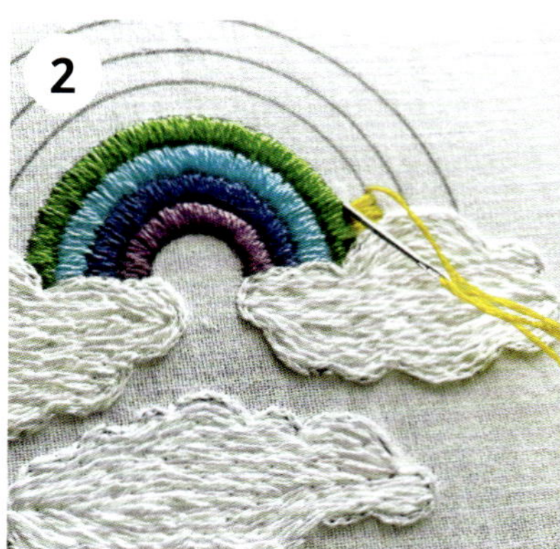

1. Start with the clouds: fill them in using split stitch filling and B5200, working the rows of stitches to follow the contours of the shapes.
2. For the rainbow, starting with the smallest arc at the base, fill it in with satin stitch using 553. For the next arc, use 798, followed by 3846, and so on, upwards, with 702, 444, 741 and finally 891. Keep all the stitches neat and close together.

Motif 98:
Fleur de Lys

This ornamental shape, consisting of three 'petals', a stalk and a crossbar, is a heraldic symbol that resembles a stylized lily flower or perhaps an iris. Some people even interpret it as a spearhead.

Thread colours

- 553 grape
- 210 lilac
- 783 mustard
- 444 yellow

Use two strands of thread throughout.

1. Working in padded satin stitch, fill in the crossbar with 553.
2. Each petal is divided into two: fill in the left-hand section of each with 210 and the right-hand section with 783. (You can use regular satin stitch or padded satin stitch, depending on the effect you wish to achieve.)
3. Now work a satin stitch border all round, using 783.
4. Finally, embroider a French knot on each marked dot, using 444.

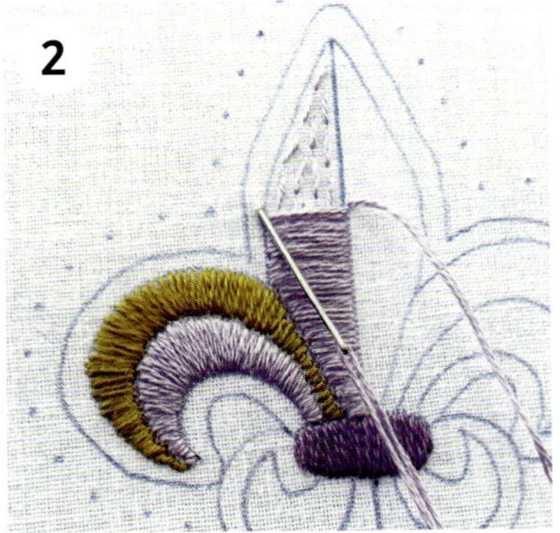

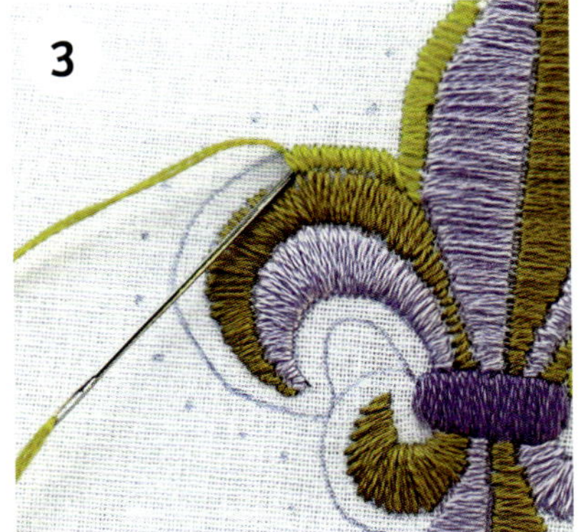

Creative ideas

The fleur de lys is mostly associated with France, as Louis VII first used it on his royal seal in the twelfth century. However, it's not exclusively French: it is used in some other European nations, too. It would make an excellent repeat pattern on a cushion cover.

Motif 99:
Moon

The moon is a popular motif; in this case, it has a sleepy face. If you choose simple outlining stitches, it is very quick and easy to embroider.

Thread colours

- 799 cornflower
- 642 stone
- 3806 fuchsia
- 444 yellow

Use two strands of thread throughout.

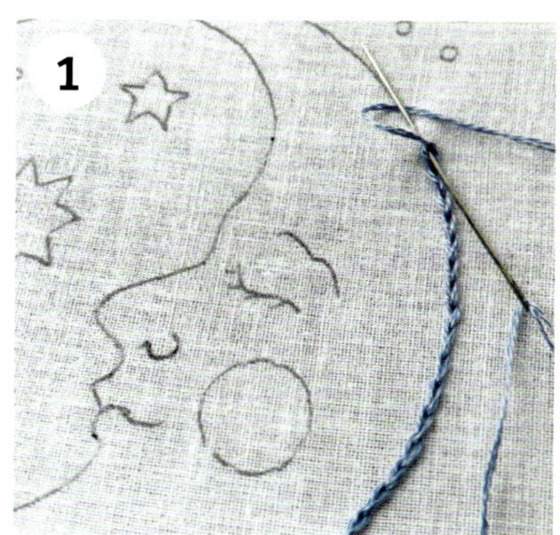

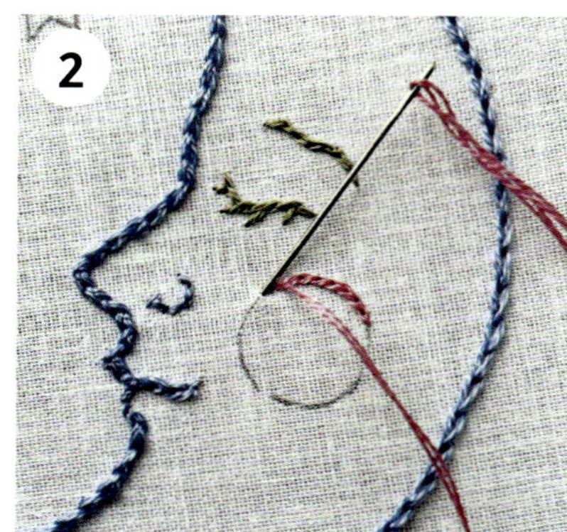

1. Outline the moon in 799, using chain stitch and keeping the stitches small, neat and even.
2. With the same colour, outline the nostril in split stitch. Using split stitch again, define the eye and eyebrow in 642 and the round cheek in 3806.
3. For the stars, use 444 and satin stitch to fill in each one, working from the outside to the centre. Fill in the small celestial round shapes with satin stitch straight across.

Creative ideas

This motif would look delightful on a pillowcase or blanket for a baby. You could add more stars to extend the embroidery over a larger area.

Motif 100:
Sun

The sun, when used as a decorative motif, can signify a number of things, including life, light, warmth, power and positivity.

Thread colours

- 3846 aqua
- B5200 white
- 760 salmon
- 307 buttermilk
- 642 stone
- 444 yellow
- 742 apricot

Use two strands of thread throughout.

1. Using satin stitch, fill in the eye centres with 3846 and the white of each eye with B5200. Also fill in the mouth with 760.
2. Change to 307 and split stitch filling, and fill in the whole face – the central circle – starting by going around the outline then following the contours.
3. Thread your needle with 642 and go over the outlines of the features: eyebrows, nose, eyes and cheeks.
4. Using 444 and satin stitch, fill in the sun's rays, working short stitches across the shapes. Then, working stitches in the other direction, fill in the shapes in between using 742.

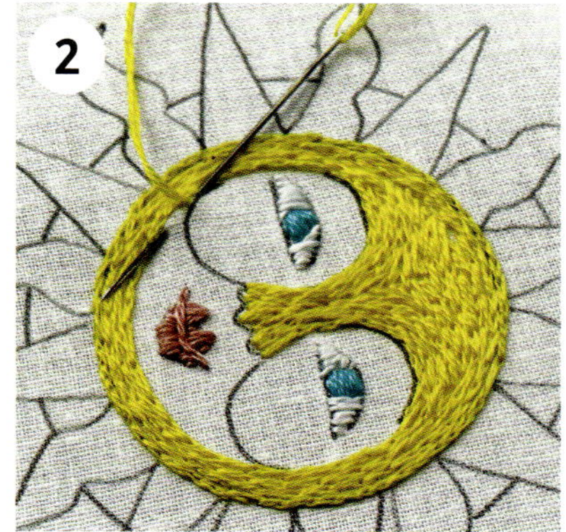

Index

First published 2025 by
Guild of Master Craftsman Publications Ltd, Castle Place,
166 High Street, Lewes, East Sussex, BN7 1XU, UK
www.gmcbooks.com

ISBN 978 1 78494 705 7

The EEA authorised representative is Authorised Rep Compliance Ltd.
Ground Floor, 71 Baggot Street Lower, Dublin, DO2 P593, Ireland
www.arccompliance.com

A catalogue record for this book is available from the British Library.

Publisher Jonathan Bailey
Production Jim Bulley
Senior Project Editor Tom Kitch
Design Manager Robin Shields
Editor Theresa Bebbington
Designer Ellie Smith
Illustrations Martin Woodward

Colour origination by GMC Reprographics
Printed and bound in China

Hoop photograph (front cover and page 10) © Pixel-Shot/Shutterstock

To order a book, contact:
GMC Publications Ltd
Castle Place, 166 High Street,
Lewes, East Sussex, BN7 1XU,
United Kingdom
Tel: +44 (0)1273 488005
www.gmcbooks.com